INVESTMENT WISDOM

750 Quotes from 50 Legendary Investors

Mariusz Skonieczny with
Quoteswise.com

Quote Publishing

MISHAWAKA, INDIANA

Quote Publishing
1202 Far Pond Cir
Mishawaka, IN 46544

Investment Wisdom/Mariusz Skonieczny with Quoteswise.com. -- 1st ed.
ISBN 978-0-692-59393-6

We recognized early on that very smart people do very dumb things, and we wanted to know why and who, so we could avoid them.

—CHARLIE MUNGER

CONTENTS

PREFACE

On May 17, 1792, 24 New York City stockbrokers and merchants gathered under a buttonwood tree to sign an agreement that they would trade only with each other at a commission rate of 0.25%. This agreement was the foundation for what would later become the largest and most powerful exchange in the world—the New York Stock Exchange. Though the stock market has actually been around for hundreds of years, the version we know today began to form around this time and, naturally, a number of extraordinary investors have emerged. Fortunately, many of them share their knowledge through speeches, books, and letters to shareholders.

To create this book, we compiled some of the best quotes from 50 investors who have distinguished themselves in the world of investing. Their insight and intuition come to life through their words, and we can tap into their knowledge to avoid the same mistakes. Instead of focusing on just the most popular ones, like Warren Buffett, we sought out a variety—some names may be familiar, but many are unknown to most investors. Some had privileged backgrounds while others scraped their way to the top. Some began investing as children while others found it as a second career. Some traveled all over the world to conduct their research while others never left the office.

Nevertheless, nearly all of them are bargain hunters, contrarians, and independent thinkers. They have learned from failure to achieve success. Quotes can convey so much wisdom in so few words. You will see that these words of wisdom never grow old. Some are so perceptive and carefully thought out that the more you read them, the more you will learn from them. With that being said, we hope that you will enjoy the journey.

BILL ACKMAN

Bill Ackman is the founder of Pershing Square Capital Management, a Manhattan-based activist hedge fund. He was born in 1966 in Chappaqua, New York, and graduated with a bachelor's degree in social studies from Harvard College in 1988. In 1992, he graduated with an MBA from Harvard Business School.

Ackman's investment career started well, but in 1997, he made an investment that would later be the undoing of his firm. Right after receiving his MBA, he co-founded the investment firm Gotham Partners with his friend, David Berkowitz, in 1992. At first, the firm did well, generating respectable returns. However, a decade later, it was forced to close mainly due to a bad investment in an operator of golf courses and an investigation of its trading practices by New York Attorney General Eliot Spitzer. The investigation did not find any wrongdoing.

Although the Gotham fiasco was a big embarrassment, it did not detour Ackman from eventually succeeding. In 2003, he founded Pershing Square Capital Management with his own funds and $50 million from Leucadia National Corporation. Because of its successful investment record, as of the end of 2014, Pershing Square managed over $18 billion, making Ackman a billionaire.

In order to be successful, you have to make sure
that being rejected doesn't bother you at all.

*Here I am, I own 25 percent of the company.
I'm offering to help. Their stock is trading for
pennies and they won't let me on the board?*

We want a business that sells a product or a service that people need
and is somewhat unique. And they have a loyalty to some sort of
brand or product and people are willing to pay a premium for that.

The benefit of short sellers to the markets is they're sort of the
canary in the coal mine. ... They are the early warning signal about
a problem in the business, a problem in the capital markets.

In the investing business, you need [a] high degree of confidence
but you also need a high degree of humbleness and you have to
balance those two. ... Humbleness comes from mistakes.

Investing is one of the few things you can learn on your own.

You should think more about what you're paying versus what the business is worth.
As opposed to what you're paying versus what they're going to earn next quarter.

We seek to identify companies which offer a high degree of predictability in their businesses and are relatively immune to extrinsic factors like fluctuations in commodity prices, interest rates, and the economic cycle. Often, we are not capable of predicting a business' earnings power over an extended period of time. These investments typically end up in the "Don't Know" pile.

We are always willing to sell an existing holding at a profit or a loss, if we can find a better use for the funds.

To be a very successful investor, you have to be able to avoid some natural human tendencies to follow the herd. The stock market is going down every day—your natural tendency is to want to sell. And the stock market is actually going up every day—your tendency is to want to buy. So, in bubbles you probably should be a seller. In busts, you should probably be a buyer. You have to have that kind of a discipline, you have to have a stomach to withstand the volatility of the stock market.

You want a product to be unique. You don't want it to be a commodity that everyone else can sell. Because when you sell a commodity—anyone can sell it and they can sell it at a better price and it's very hard to make a profit doing that.

What's kept me intrigued is that it is one of the few jobs where every day you can study something new. You are constantly learning about new businesses, new situations, new management teams, new issues. So, it's infinitely challenging. ... The world and the stock market are obviously dynamic places.

Investing is not a business where every investment is profitable.

LEE AINSLIE

Lee Ainslie is the founder and managing partner of Maverick Capital, a long/short hedge fund. Born in 1964 in Alexandria, Virginia, he became interested in investing in eighth grade. He enjoyed computer programming, and a high school teacher asked if he could develop a program for an investment club to track which stocks had been chosen by which students. While working on it, he became interested and asked to join the club even though he was not in high school yet.

Even though he was introduced to investing at an early age, he did not pursue a bachelor's degree in it. Instead, he earned an engineering degree from the University of Virginia in 1986. He returned to the investment field when he went to the University of North Carolina for its MBA program. This is where he met legendary investor Julian Robertson who, at that time, was on UNC's board of trustees. The two men got to know each other pretty well after Ainslie was asked to work on a couple of projects with the board. Ainslie and Robertson spent a lot of time talking about stocks. Upon graduating from UNC in 1990, Robertson asked Ainslie to join his firm, Tiger Management. This is where he built his foundation in value investing. However, while many of his picks would be considered value stocks, he doesn't necessarily call himself a value investor. He also invests in growth stocks that others might consider expensive, and he doesn't assume that an undervalued stock will appreciate just because it should.

When Ainslie was only 28 years old, he was approached by a wealthy family to branch out on his own. At first, he was reluctant because he liked his job and was treated well there. However, he eventually gave in and started Maverick Capital in 1993 with $38 million of seeded capital. Today, Maverick Capital manages several billion dollars.

If a week goes by that I haven't learned something
new, then that is really a wasted week.

It's not impossible, but the odds are against you if your view is the same as everyone
else's because that view is probably already reflected in a stock's valuation.

At the time of maximum pain, you need to maintain your discipline.

We spend an inordinate amount of time trying to understand
the quality, ability, and motivation of a management team.

We have made the mistake more than once of not investing in a company with a
great management team because of valuation concerns—only to look back a
year later and realize we missed an opportunity because the management team
made intelligent, strategic decisions that had a significant impact.

A short seller is really the only guaranteed buyer that a company has.

Evaluating people and evaluating securities are two different skills.

When a business is generating a strong return on capital
and the cash flow stream can be reinvested effectively, then
we may be able to own that stock for several years.

While we place great emphasis on valuation in our
investment decisions, valuation alone should never be
the driver of either a long or a short investment.

*The most critical factor that we're trying to
evaluate is the quality of management —
their intelligence, competitiveness and,
most importantly, their desire to create
shareholder value.*

I believe that a successful investor must be very comfortable with a number of
different valuation methodologies and have the wisdom to recognize which
valuation approach is going to be the most relevant in different situations.

When we evaluate a management team, we're much more focused on analyzing past
decisions and actions than simply reviewing their responses to our questions.

BERNARD BARUCH

Bernard Baruch is one of the most legendary investors. He was born in 1870 and died in 1965. Even after his death, many investors aspire to be like him and quote him widely.

During the first 10 years of his life, he lived in the small town of Camden, South Carolina. In 1881, his family moved to New York City, and in 1889, he graduated from the tuition-free College of the City of New York (now known as the City College of New York). One of his first jobs was as an "office boy"—a runner and comparison clerk who also fetched sandwiches and filled inkstands. He worked his way up selling semi-defunct rail lines.

In 1897, Baruch successfully bet that Congress would vote to protect American sugar. He invested $300 and made a profit of $60,000. Of the proceeds, he spent $19,000 on something he had longed for—a seat on the stock exchange. However, he impulsively offered it to his actor brother, who accepted it. After hours of agonizing, he resolved to buy another for himself. It was two years before he was able to do so, and the price had risen to $39,000.

In 1903, Baruch went into business for himself, investing and speculating with his own money. He made a name for himself, but once World War I began, he switched his focus to advocating for war preparation. From 1917 on, he was a public servant, working many assignments including heading the War Industries Board. He acted as an advisor to all nine US presidents who served from 1916 through 1965—Woodrow Wilson to Lyndon B. Johnson.

In 1929, Baruch asked Benjamin Graham, who was in his mid-30s, to be his business partner. Graham declined because he had just completed a year where he had yielded a personal net profit of more than $600,000 and saw no reason to be Baruch's junior partner, despite his prestige.

The longer I operated in Wall Street the more distrustful I became of tips and "inside" information of every kind. Given time, I believe that inside information can break the Bank of England or the United States Treasury.

Repeatedly, in my market operations I have sold a stock while it still was rising—and that has been one reason why I have held on to my fortune.

It is far more difficult ... to know when to sell a stock than when to buy.

Don't try to buy at the bottom and sell at the top. This can't be done—except by liars.

The main reason why money is lost in stock speculations is not because Wall Street is dishonest, but because so many people persist in thinking that you can make money without working for it and that the stock exchange is the place where this miracle can be performed.

Vote for the man who promises least; he'll be the least disappointing.

It is one thing to make money and another thing to keep it. In fact, making money is often easier than keeping it.

A man with no special pipeline of information will study the economic facts of a situation and will act coldly on that basis. Give the same man inside information and he feels himself so much smarter than other people that he will disregard the most evident facts.

BRUCE BERKOWITZ

Bruce Berkowitz is the founder of Fairholme Capital Management, and the Fairholme Fund, a mutual fund. He is very well known in value investing circles for his "Ignore the Crowd" motto. Berkowitz runs a concentrated portfolio, and as a result, his fund experiences wide volatility. Because of this, his popularity with his investors and the media swings wildly as well.

Berkowitz and Fairholme do not employ any full-time teams of research analysts. He does all the investing himself. Instead, he hires consultants and asks them to "kill the company." If they cannot figure out how to kill it, then he might consider the company to be a worthwhile investment.

Born in 1958 and raised in Chelsea, Massachusetts, his father was a part-time taxi driver and bookmaker in addition to running a corner grocery store. Berkowitz missed two months of high school at the age of 15 to take over the bookie operation while his father recovered from a heart attack.

Berkowitz earned his bachelor's degree in economics from the University of Massachusetts in 1980. After graduation, he and his wife both worked for the Strategic Planning Institute in Cambridge, Massachusetts, but were transferred to London. After two years, he joined Merrill Lynch in London. He thought that he could do a better job than his broker did. In 1986, he accepted a job with Lehman

Brothers in London, and in 1989 he transferred to the company's New Jersey office. Finally, in 1997, he ventured out on his own to start Fairholme Capital Management, named after the street on which he lived, and in 1999, he created the Fairholme Fund.

At some point in a business cycle, one has to get greedy. And the time to get greedy is when everybody's running for the hills with fear.

There are two ways to invest: you can predict or you can react.

Ignore the crowd.

My definition of skill is knowing when you're lucky and taking advantage of that luck.

Cash is the equivalent of financial Valium. It keeps you cool, calm and collected.

Cash is really valuable when no one has it.

You need only a few good ideas in a lifetime to become wealthier than you ever thought possible.

Great investors never run out of cash. We always want to have a lot of cash.

We look at companies, count the cash, and then try to kill the company. ... We spend a lot of time thinking about what could go wrong with a company. ... We try every which way to kill our best ideas. If we can't kill it, maybe we're onto something.

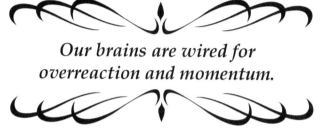

Our brains are wired for overreaction and momentum.

If you go with companies that are prepared for difficult times, especially if they're linked to managers who are engineered for difficult times, then you almost want those times because they plant the seeds of greatness.

We spend a lot of time on mistakes and asking why we make them. It's great for the investment process.

If the company buys back undervalued stock, selling shareholders suffer while long-term shareholders benefit. If the company buys its stock at inflated prices, sellers benefit and long-term holders lose out. Value investors, having a long-term orientation, generally look for companies that consistently repurchase their stocks during periods of undervaluation.

Identifying a company with a big cash stash and the ability to generate more is a great start. But the cash doesn't do the shareholder any good unless management makes smart investments with it, or returns it to its owners via dividends or share buybacks.

We always have a lot of cash. Cash becomes extremely valuable when few have it and cash in some ways is a financial Valium. It allows us to deal with extremely stressful times; it allows us to take advantage of cheap prices without having to sell anything. It gives our shareholders liquidity, so we always have a lot of cash, and thankfully, we have great, great shareholders who have stayed the course with us.

I've always suffered from premature accumulation. ... I've always bought too early and felt the pain of buying too early. But the trick is not running out of cash.

CARSON BLOCK

Carson Block was a relatively unknown short seller who put himself on the map overnight in June 2010 by releasing a paper on a Chinese company, Orient Paper, that he thought was a fraud. He sent it to only a few friends and colleagues and was shocked when the stock, which was trading for more than $8 per share, dropped to around $4 per share within 48 hours of the release of the report.

He became known for publicly challenging the accounting practices of several Chinese companies that trade on North American stock exchanges and betting against them with his own money. He founded Muddy Waters Research, which publishes reports on three areas of interest: business fraud, accounting fraud, and fundamental problems. The firm has less than 10 employees and releases investment research free of charge. It makes money by trading its principals' own capital.

Block was born in 1976 and grew up in Summit, New Jersey. His interest in Asia began when he spent a month in Japan at the age of 15. He graduated from the University of Southern California, where he studied business, finance, and Chinese, and he has a law degree from the Illinois Institute of Technology. He worked as a lawyer in Shanghai, and later, was based in Hong Kong. However, he had to relocate to California due to death threats.

Audits of public companies are not designed to detect fraud. Auditing standards presume that company documents are genuine and management does not make misrepresentations about their numbers.

When you're in this business of short selling, you really do your homework.

We take two to three months to look at a company. The conventional investment-bank/analyst model doesn't really support doing that depth of research.

The Six Rules of China Due Diligence. Rule #1 – Approach the company as a potential customer does. Rule #2 – Take all company-provided introductions with a grain of salt. Rule #3 – Try to construct your own fraud scenario. Rule #4 – Forget about the paper. Focus on the operations. Rule #5 – Always speak with competitors. Rule #6 – Do not delegate.

Big-name auditors aren't that well equipped to protect investors against managements who are determined to commit fraud.

You have to look at the operation itself. How much does the output seem to be, how much material is moving into and out of the factory, does the office seem to be a hive of activity, how many employees can you count, what is the square footage of the facilities? These are all basic questions one should concern themselves with during site visits.

Many competitors will be reluctant to speak openly at first about a fraudulent competitor if they know you're a potential investor in the fraudulent company. However, if you're a potential customer who is shopping around for a vendor, it can be a different story.

Your biggest fear, when you short a stock, is a squeeze. And one way to get squeezed is to have a bunch of other people in the short so that when they try to cover, it pushes the stock up and you start losing money.

One thing that's true of investing whether you're on the long side or short side: You could be right, but still not make money. That happens occasionally.

When a company pays such a high price for an acquisition, we always think about possible ulterior motivations. We have observed that when some companies see organic growth starting to decelerate, they make significant acquisitions (in number, size, or both) because this tends to obscure the organic growth picture.

Audits are generally performed from pre-constructed checklists that are used in thousands of public company audits throughout the world. These checklists incorporate the standard presumption of honesty. As a result, auditors are not visiting a company's customers to make sure revenue is accurate nor are they visiting suppliers to confirm whether the company's volumes match up with the financials they are reporting. Auditors also do not review government files to confirm that a company's filings with the government are the same as what they report on their financial statements.

CHARLES BRANDES

Charles Brandes is the founder and chairman of Brandes Investment Partners, and has been in the investment business since 1968. He was born in 1943 in Pittsburgh, Pennsylvania, where his father worked for Gulf Oil. In 1965, he earned his bachelor's degree in economics from Bucknell University.

Brandes has always seen himself as a contrarian, choosing San Diego—a community like his hometown of Pittsburgh—over Wall Street despite the lack of financial services firms. He moved there to pursue graduate studies at San Diego State University, and his first job was as a stockbroker and analyst at Roberts, Scott and Company in La Jolla. One day, an older gentleman walked into the office and it was Benjamin Graham. After meeting Graham, Brandes was sold on value investing and has practiced it ever since. It was the only investment philosophy that made sense to him.

In 1974, the markets experienced a severe bear market and, seeing an opportunity to buy a lot of companies on the cheap, he founded Brandes Investment Partners. Regarding his investment strategy, he has said that he does not like to copy other value investors because he believes that indicates a lack of conviction. He is the author of the book *Brandes on Value: The Independent Investor*.

The stock market is inherently misleading. Doing what everybody else is doing can often be wrong.

They find themselves switching in and out of stocks, feeding the brokers instead of themselves.

Fundamentals. Fundamentals. Fundamentals.

If a president owns 20 percent or more of the shares outstanding, then we both want the same thing—increased share price. Managers tied only by salary and benefits aren't rowing the same boat as shareholders.

By choosing stocks with a substantial difference between price and value, a wide margin of safety is created. The lower the purchase price relative to value, the lower the risk. Contrary to popular belief, by decreasing risk, this method increases potential reward.

During the 1990s, momentum investing—the notion of buying stocks simply because they were going up—became popular. What each of these fads has in common is a complete disregard for fundamental value.

The distinction between investing and speculation has always been difficult to define. ... 1) Any contemplated holding period shorter than a normal business cycle (three to five years) is speculation, and 2) any purchase based on anticipated market movements or forecasting is also speculation.

Investors and speculators approach their tasks differently. Investors want to know what a business is worth and imagine themselves as owning the business as a whole. Speculators are less interested in what a business is actually worth and more concerned with what a third party will pay to own shares on a given day.

The basic ingredients necessary for your investing success. As with any endeavor, success depends on three key factors: knowledge, correct action, and patience.

Graham's essential concept of value investing remains unchanged: The shares of any sound company—even a boring, slow-growing business—are a fine investment if bought at a cheap enough price.

For many, value investing is too painstaking, too boring, and too disciplined.

Few will stay the course, since there is no excitement, no action in watching eggs that take years to come to a boil.

Patience is necessary if large and enduring profits are to be made from equity investments. Put another way, it is often easier to tell what will happen to the price of a security than when it will happen.

High expectations are difficult to meet.

The basic fundamental thing about investing and especially value investors is number one: It's a very obvious, very simple thing to do. There's nothing terribly complicated about being a value investor, number one. Number two, in actual practice it becomes extremely difficult; of course if it was all that easy, everybody would be doing it and there wouldn't be value stocks out there anymore.

The market is crazy, most of the time. You should only think about the fundamentals of the investment that you are actually making and whether that makes sense over a long period of time.

Most people get involved in thinking and getting confused about the difference between investment and speculation.

The bottom line of value investing ... is to make money.

RON BRIERLEY

Ron Brierley is a New Zealand investor who was born in 1937 in Wellington. He worked for an insurance company after he finished school and studied accounting part time at Victoria University. At the age of 19, he began writing a newsletter, *New Zealand Stocks and Shares*. In order to build his subscriber base, he would ask for a list of shareholders every time he researched a company and send his tip sheet unsolicited, along with a bill, to all of them. With this method, he was able to get a rate of two subscribers out of 100.

A stamp trader and cricket enthusiast, he became known as a corporate raider, which is what activist investors used to be called. In 1961, he founded R.A. Brierley Investments, Ltd., in order to acquire substantial holdings in "dead" public companies that were rich in assets but poor in earnings. At the time, there were many companies like this in New Zealand. Also, there was no effective regulation regarding takeovers and insider trading. As an activist, he forced companies to make changes that would benefit shareholders, such as selling underperforming assets.

Brierley Investments, Ltd. (BIL), grew to become the largest company on the New Zealand Stock Exchange. In the 1970s and 1980s, the firm was one of the most feared corporate raiders, and investors hung on to every word that came out of Brierley's mouth. Many tried to emulate him the way investors copy Warren Buffett.

However, following the 1987 stock market crash, Brierley was ousted as the chairman of BIL but remained on the board. He was also the head of two other companies, Industrial Equity Limited, BIL's counterpart in Australia, and Guinness Peat Group, which he took control of in the early 1990s.

To make money fast, make it slowly.

In every cycle, there's an increasing number of people who forget that there were previous cycles, and they genuinely believe that share prices are forever only going to go up.

If you own the value, the unlocking is secondary. Once you own something, if the value is there, you might have to rack your brains to find a solution, but it is better than finding there is no value to unlock.

I think one just has to ride with the ups and downs of an economy over the long term.

I'm much more interested in real values than market values.

It's a great pity when well-managed companies, which are genuinely trying to maximize shareholder values, do get diverted into the other nonsense, the absolute nonsense, of so-called poison pills.

My strength was to research companies and to reach a conclusion that their assets were worth more than their sharemarket price and to work out ways to exploit that to our own advantage in the most effective way. That was my strength. It was my only strength, and I'd have to say from my point of view, that I never really wavered from that in 40 years. I'm sitting here in an office in London applying the same principles as I did in the 1960s.

I have no faith in large boards of directors, which tend to be at the top of a bureaucracy rather than a commercial organization.

What triggered my interest [in the stock market] was the desire to make some money and the sharemarket seemed to be the purest way to do so. Investing in the market had a certain romantic appeal, but it was interesting as well. It just had all the ingredients that one was looking for in a business sense.

Balance sheet values can't be accepted in terms of what they say. You've got to make your own assessment.

The company was dirt cheap, but nobody wanted to know about it. That type of company proved to be an absolute gold mine for me.

Corporate governance—it's a fancy term, but the principles of corporate governance have always been there, and it's a very basic and natural discipline; it's not something that requires manuals and lots of rule books. I think the emphasis on so-called corporate governance is so far over the top it's doing a disservice to shareholders, rather than assisting them. It's tending to turn companies from entrepreneurial entities into bureaucratic entities.

The companies that talk loudest about corporate governance and fill up their annual reports with the most number of pages are those that are most likely to be cheating their shareholders behind the scenes.

I had one good idea. ... It was a good idea 50 years ago and it's still a good idea today. That was that some companies were worth more dead than alive. That sounds a bit stark, but that's the basic principle.

CHRISTOPHER H. BROWNE

Christopher H. Browne was a famous value investor who was born in 1946 and died at the age of 62 in 2009. He believed that value investing was the stress-free way to investment success, and he intended to continue working until he was at least 90.

In 1969, he graduated from the University of Pennsylvania with a bachelor's degree in history. His investing career began at Tweedy, Browne and Company, which was founded by his father, Howard S. Browne, and Bill Tweedy. One day in June 1969, he walked into their offices to borrow $5 from his father for a train ride home, and his father's partner, Ed Anderson, introduced him to value investing and hired him for the summer. Browne never left and ended up working there for 40 years.

Tweedy, Browne and Company was a "thrift-shop-style" brokerage company that was used by both Benjamin Graham and Warren Buffett. It was through this company that Buffett bought a controlling interest in Berkshire Hathaway in 1965. Browne was the person that recorded trades in Berkshire Hathaway, which in 1969, were $25 per share. Later, the company transformed itself into a money management firm which specialized in investing in unpopular stocks at cheap prices. In other words, he allocated capital following the same philosophy as Graham and Buffett. Browne was also the author of *The Little Book of Value Investing*.

Value investors are more like farmers. They plant seeds and wait for the crops to grow. If the corn is a little late in starting because of cold weather, they don't tear up the fields and plant something else. No, they just sit back and wait patiently for the corn to pop out of the ground, confident that it will eventually sprout.

Value investing is the stress-free route to investment success.

> Value investing is straightforward; it does not require a superhuman set of brain cells. The average person can understand the logic of it all. Buy a dollar for 60 cents from some unsuspecting seller and wait until the person wants it back for a dollar.

Sex sells even in the stock market, and everyone wants to own the latest sexy issue. Value stocks are about as exciting as watching the grass grow. But have you ever noticed just how much your grass grows in a week?

Most people seek immediate gratification in almost everything they do, including investing. When most investors buy a stock, they expect it to go up immediately. If it doesn't, they sell it and buy something else.

When stocks climb, Wall Street research reports scream BUY. When stocks fall, the experts tell us to HOLD when they really mean SELL. (Sell is considered impolite in the world of stocks except under the most extreme circumstances). Everyone seems to think they should buy stocks that are rising and sell those that are falling.

It's time in the market,
not market timing, that counts.

There is nothing wrong with owning great businesses that can grow at fast rates. The fault in this approach lies in the price that investors pay.

Insiders are usually investors, not traders.

My best friend in the whole world when it comes to building my inventory of value investing opportunities is the no-thank-you pile. If there is something you do not understand or are not comfortable with, in the no-thank-you pile it should go.

A strong balance sheet is a good indicator of a company's stamina, its ability to survive when the going gets tough.

A lot of reputedly smart professional analysts could not figure out Enron's income statement, but that did not stop them from becoming big fans of the stock.

Isales can be grown at no additional cost, every dollar goes right to bottom-line profits. If, however, a company has to hire additional salespeople, build new plants, or add additional shipping costs to gain growth, the increased sales will not all translate into bottom-line profit.

Long term, value investing is like flying from New York to Los Angeles. While you may encounter some air turbulence over Kansas, if your plane is in good shape, there is no reason to bail out. You will eventually reach your destination safely, and probably even on time. The same goes for investing.

Patience is sometimes the hardest part of using the value approach. When I find a stock that sells for 50 percent of what I have determined it is worth, my job is basically done. Now, it is up to the stock. It may move up toward its real worth today, next week, or next year. It may trade sideways for five years and then quadruple in price. There is simply no way to know when a particular stock will appreciate.

WARREN BUFFETT

Warren Buffett does not need an introduction. He is the most famous investor in the world. If there was a picture in the dictionary describing value investing, it would be of Warren Buffett. Currently, he is the chairman, CEO, and largest shareholder of Berkshire Hathaway. He is called the "Oracle of Omaha."

The future is never clear. You pay a very high price in the stock market for a cheery consensus. Uncertainty is the friend of the buyer of long-term values.

Price is what you pay, value is what you get.

I never attempt to make money on the stock market. I buy on the assumption that they could close the market the next day and not reopen it for five years. As far as you are concerned, the stock market does not exist. Ignore it. Much success can be attributed to inactivity. Most investors cannot resist the temptation to constantly buy and sell.

We think diversification, as practiced generally, makes very little sense for anyone who knows what they are doing. Diversification serves as protection against ignorance.

Time is the friend of the wonderful business, the enemy of the mediocre. You might think this principle is obvious, but I had to learn it the hard way. ... It is far better to buy a wonderful company at a fair price than a fair company at a wonderful price. Charlie understood this early; I was a slow learner. But now, when buying companies or common stocks, we look for first-class businesses accompanied by first class managements. That leads right into a related lesson: Good jockeys will do well on good horses but not on broken-down nags.

Rule number 1: Don't lose money.
Rule number 2: Don't forget rule number one.
Rule number 3: Don't go into debt.

You can't do well investing unless you think independently. And the truth is, you are neither right nor wrong because people agree with you. You're right because your facts and reasoning are right. In the end, that's what counts.

Cash combined with courage in a crisis is priceless.

The inescapable fact is that the value of an asset, whatever its character, cannot over the long term grow faster than its earnings.

The market is there only as a reference point to see if anybody is offering to do anything foolish. When we invest in stocks, we invest in businesses.

Charlie and I have not learned how to solve difficult business problems. What we have learned is to avoid them.

There is also another alternative: Don't do anything. More fortunes are made by sitting on good securities for years at a time than by active trading.

The stock market is a no-called strike game. You don't have to swing at everything—you can wait for your pitch. The problem when you're a money manager is that your fans keep yelling, "Swing, you bum!"

The most common cause of low prices is pessimism—sometimes pervasive, sometimes specific to a company or industry. We want to do business in such an environment, not because we like pessimism but because we like the prices it produces. It's optimism that is the enemy of the rational buyer.

I never talk to brokers or analysts. Wall Street is the only place that people who ride to work in a Rolls Royce get advice from those who take the subway.

A parent company that owns a subsidiary with superb long-term economics will not sell the company's "crown jewel". Yet this same CEO will impulsively sell stocks in his personal portfolio with little more logic than "You can't go broke taking a profit." In our view, what makes sense in business also makes sense in stocks. An investor should ordinarily hold a small piece of an outstanding business with the same tenacity that an owner would exhibit if he owned all of that business.

———————————※———————————

I'd be a bum on the street with a tin cup if the markets were always efficient.

Mr. Market is there to serve you, not to guide you. ... It will be disastrous if you fall under his influence.

In a business selling a commodity-type product, it's impossible to be a lot smarter than your dumbest competitor.

———————————※———————————

The trick is, when there is nothing to do, do nothing.

———————————※———————————

It's only when the tide goes out that you learn who's been swimming naked.

———————————※———————————

A stock doesn't know you own it.

Be fearful when others are greedy, and greedy when others are fearful.

Most people get interested in stocks when everyone else is. The time to get interested is when no one else is. You can't buy what is popular and do well.

I am a better investor because I am a businessman, and a better businessman because I am an investor.

The fact that people will be full of greed, fear, or folly is predictable. The sequence is not predictable.

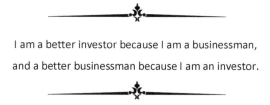

You should invest in a business that even a fool can run, because someday a fool will.

All there is to investing is picking good stocks at good times and staying with them as long as they remain good companies.

When a management with a reputation for brilliance tackles a business with a reputation for poor fundamental economics, it is the reputation of the business that remains intact.

Our favorite holding period is forever.

It is not that we don't understand a technology business or its product. The reason we don't invest is because we can't understand the predictability of the economics 10 years hence.

We select our marketable equity securities in much the same way we
would evaluate a business for acquisition in its entirety.
We want the business to be one
a) that we understand,
b) with favorable long-term prospects,
c) operated by honest and competent people, and
d) available at a very attractive price.

*If you cannot control your emotions,
you cannot control your money.*

JIM CHANOS

Jim Chanos is a famous short seller who revealed fraud at Enron and WorldCom. He was born in 1958 in Milwaukee, Wisconsin, to a Greek immigrant family. In 1980, he graduated from Yale University with a degree in economics and political science. He is the founder of Kynikos Associates, a New York City registered investment advisor specializing in short selling. The word cynic is derived from the Greek word Kynikos.

To achieve investment success, he employs an extremely detailed investment strategy that he describes as "intensive research into stocks." In 2011, International Business Times named Chanos the best short seller in the world.

He became interested in short selling after analyzing Baldwin-United Corporation at his first job. Though he was absolutely right about the company's fraudulent activities, the experience was extremely painful. After recommending that investors short sell the stock, the price doubled and clients lost money. He almost lost his job. It took some time for the market to finally catch up to what he already knew, but eventually, he was proven right.

In both the Baldwin-United and Enron cases, all the information that led Chanos to short the stock was publicly available, or as he put it, "hiding in plain sight" (Weiss, 68). In one instance, it was clear that one of his critics had not even looked at the financial records. Chanos has what he calls the "Rule of Three," meaning that if you read a financial disclosure three times and still cannot understand it, the obscurity is intentional (Weiss, 64).

Short sellers are the professional skeptics who look past the hype to gauge the true value of a stock.

When it comes to investigating corporate fraud, it's the short sellers who are the detectives, while all too often our regulators practice archaeology.

At the end of the day, the language of business is numbers. ... If you're not very comfortable with understanding how companies can play games with their financial statements using GAAP accounting, you're never going to be a good short seller. That's just the bottom line.

Good short sellers have something in the DNA. Or, maybe we were dropped on our heads as babies.

As an analyst, you have to be very comfortable with the balance sheet, flow of funds statement, and very comfortable reading the footnotes. That's blocking and tackling 101.

Wall Street always attacks naysayers during the boom. Problems do not go away by silencing critics.

PETER CUNDILL

Peter Cundill was a Canadian value investor. He was born in Montreal, Québec, in 1938 and died in 2011. At an early age, he showed an interest in investing, and his father, who had a gambling problem and saw investing as another way to gamble, was afraid his son would have the same trouble. He thought it would be better if his son at least had professional qualifications in the field. As a result, Cundill studied commerce at McGill University and became a chartered accountant.

In 1959, he spent his summer vacation working as an "office boy" for Wood Gundy, an investment banking and brokerage firm where his uncle, Pete Scott, was a partner and later a chairman. During that summer he bought his first stock, which was that of a speculative mining company. Within 48 hours, he had lost his entire investment. He never forgot that experience.

In 1960, Cundill graduated from McGill with a bachelor's degree and worked for several firms before starting his own in 1977. His investment style was inspired by Benjamin Graham. However, he didn't learn about him until he was 35. During a flight to Vancouver in 1973, he read the book *Supermoney* by George Goodman (a.k.a. Adam Smith) and learned not only about Graham but also about Buffett, and "the margin of safety." After that, he became one of the best net-net investors. However, unlike Graham, instead of buying lots

RAY DALIO

Ray Dalio is the founder of Bridgewater Associates, the world's biggest hedge fund firm. He was born in 1949 in Jackson Heights, Queens, New York. Inspired by golfers at the club where he caddied, Dalio started investing at the age of 12 and was profitable on his first try, purchasing the stock of Northeast Airlines and seeing it triple after the company merged with another company. It gave him the impression that investing was an easy game, but it didn't take long before he lost money. He earned his bachelor's degree in finance from Long Island University in 1971 and his MBA from Harvard University in 1973.

Before founding Bridgewater Associates out of a spare bedroom in his apartment in 1975, he worked on the floor of the New York Stock Exchange, and began investing in commodity futures. Dalio is a macro investor, betting on big-picture economic trends and specializing in the bond and currency markets. He is also known for imposing an open, candid culture within his firm that runs counter to the typical Wall Street scene. He calls his philosophy radical transparency, meaning that in the interest of improvement, he and his employees are expected to speak openly about their own and other's mistakes and weaknesses; however, some consider it hypercritical. He tapes every meeting at the firm.

Dalio was forever changed when he saw the stock market rally after Nixon's August 1971 announcement that the dollar would no longer be backed by gold. He had been sure it would tank, so he decided to study cases of currency devaluation throughout history to understand what had happened. In 2007, he correctly predicted the global financial crisis. Dalio published a 123-page manifesto, *Principles*, in which he laid out his philosophies on investing, employee management, and life. He also created an animated video called *How the Economic Machine Works*.

The biggest mistake in investing is believing the last three years is representative of what the next three years is going to be like.

I think anybody who is a great investor, a good investor, a successful investor has to be a person who can be both aggressive and defensive. ... You have to be able to bet. But you also have to have enough fear to have the caution. But you can't let the fear control you.

I try to limit my bets to the limited number of things I am confident in.

Using leverage is like playing Russian roulette. It means that you are inevitably going to get a bullet in the head.

The way I learn is to immerse myself in something, which prompts questions, which I answer, prompting more questions, until I reach a conclusion.

In order to make money in the market, you have to be an independent thinker. And I think also creative; you have to be willing to make mistakes.

In the markets, you can do a huge amount of work and still be wrong.

The consensus is often wrong, so I have to be an independent thinker. To make any money, you have to be right when they're wrong.

While most others seem to believe that having answers is better than having questions, I believe that having questions is better than having answers because it leads to more learning.

Without pursuing dreams, life is mundane.

I believe that pain is required to become stronger.

CHARLES DOW

Charles Dow was a prominent figure in the world of financial journalism. He was born in Sterling, Connecticut, in 1851 and died in 1902 at the age of 51, after an illness. He is known for founding *The Wall Street Journal* and creating the Dow Jones Industrial Average. He was considered to be the father of technical analysis in the West.

When Dow was six, his father died, leaving the family farm to Dow's mother. Little is known about his childhood and education other than that he left the farm at an early age and worked in a variety of jobs before becoming a journalist at the age of 18. Dow started at the *Springfield Republican* in Massachusetts and worked for several other papers before moving, around 1880, to New York City where he sought work as a reporter on mining stocks. It wasn't long before he earned a reputation as a trustworthy and skilled financial journalist.

In 1882, Dow and Edward D. Jones founded Dow, Jones and Company. Their first office was in a small room in the back of a rundown building next door to the New York Stock Exchange. Jones would dictate the news to four or five employees who would write it on carbon paper 20 pages thick. It would then be delivered by messenger boys. After one year in business, they began compiling the news into a summary sheet called the *Customers' Afternoon Letter*, which contained the daily price movements of certain stocks in addition to the financial news. At one point, Dow hired a "lady typist" in an attempt to reduce the amount of profanity used in the office.

In 1889, Dow, Jones and Company turned the two-page daily *Customers' Afternoon Letter* into a real newspaper, *The Wall Street Journal*. This publication filled the information gap and allowed regular folks to make informed investment decisions. Before that, only the rich and well connected had such information. In 1896, the calculation of price movements became known as the Dow Jones Industrial Average, which consisted of 12 stocks. Today, the Dow Jones Industrial Average consists of 30 stocks and is one of the most frequently cited market indices. The entire investment industry compares itself to this average.

Value will always work out in the course of time.

The public, as a whole, buys at the wrong time and sells at the wrong time.

The best profits in the stock market are made by people who get long or short at extremes and stay for months or years before they take their profit.

It is always safer to assume that values determine prices in the long run. Values have nothing to do with current fluctuations. A worthless stock can go up 5 points just as easily as the best, but as a result of continuous fluctuations, the good stock will gradually work up to its investment value.

It is an old saying in Wall Street that the man who begins to speculate in stocks with the intention of making a fortune usually goes broke, whereas the man who trades with a view of getting good interest on his money, sometimes gets rich.

Bull markets and bear markets run four and five years at a time.

The market is not like a balloon plunging hither and thither in the wind.

Most people however, when they talk about making money in stocks, do not mean the slow road through investments, but the shortcut by way of speculation.

This rule is to cut losses short but let profits run. It sounds very easy to follow, but is in reality difficult to observe.

The tendency with most people holding a stock which does not move for a time is to sell the stock about as soon as it begins to move, through fear that it will again become dull. This is just the time not to sell, but if anything, to buy more on the idea that other people have discovered that the price is below value.

The practical lesson is that a stock operator should not deal in stocks unless he thinks he knows their value.

People in Wall Street, even those who get very near the center of large operations, do not know what the market is going to do with any regularity or certainty.

It appears to take ordinarily five or six years for public confidence to go from the point of too little hope to the point of too much confidence and then five or six years more to get back to the condition of hopelessness.

DAVID DREMAN

David Dreman is known for contrarian investing. Actually, some say that his name is synonymous with contrarian value investing strategies. He wrote five books, with the newest one being *Contrarian Investment Strategies: The Psychological Edge*. He has been a Forbes columnist since 1979.

Dreman was born in 1936 in Winnipeg, Manitoba, Canada, and graduated from the University of Manitoba with a degree in commerce in 1957. Because his father was a high-profile trader on the Winnipeg Commodity Exchange, Dreman was introduced to financial markets early in life. His father started taking him to visit the commodity pits when he was three years old. In the late 1960s, he came to the United States for what was supposed to be about one year, but he found the American markets much more interesting and ended up staying. Before founding his investment firm, Dreman Value Management, Inc., in 1977, he did research for several companies. He began his current firm, Dreman Value Management, LLC, which is based in West Palm Beach, Florida, in 1997. At one point, he was a senior editor of the Value Line Investment Service, a research company used by many prominent investors like Warren Buffett.

In the 1990s, Dreman became known because of the success of the DWS Dreman High Return Equity Fund, a mutual fund that he began in 1988. His family of funds was bought by Kemper Financial

Services in 1995. Kemper was bought by Scudder, which was then bought by Deutsche Bank. In 2009, despite the fact that the fund had outperformed the market over the long term, his firm was fired by the board of directors. The fund's best years were in the beginning, when the total assets under management were small.

Patience is a crucial but rare investment commodity.

I buy stocks when they are really battered.

Favored stocks underperform the market, while out-of-favor companies outperform the market, but the reappraisal often happens slowly, even glacially.

Psychology, no matter how much you've studied it or think you know it, can reduce both your ego and your net worth very quickly.

It is hard to stay unaffected by psychological pressures, as I've too often found in free-falling markets. No matter how often you've been there or how much you've read, you can't escape the fear.

Most investors, whether professional or individual, even with the best of intentions, cannot follow through.

Skeptics have cheerfully suggested that blindfolded chimpanzees heavily fortified with margaritas could outperform the experts by throwing darts at the stock pages.

People, when swamped by information, may select only a small portion of the total, and reach a dramatically different conclusion than what the entire data set would suggest.

Not only do investors go wrong, they go wrong in a systematic and predictable manner. So predictable, in fact, that consistent investment strategies can be built on their mistakes.

People are not good intuitive statisticians, particularly under difficult conditions.

Well known on the street is the fear of issuing sell recommendations. Sell recommendations are only a small fraction of the buys. A company that the analyst issues a sell recommendation on will often ban him or her from further contact.

Respect the difficulty of working with a mass of information. Few of us can use it successfully. In-depth information does not translate into in-depth profits.

It is impossible, in a dynamic economy with constantly changing political, economic, industrial, and competitive conditions, to use the past the estimate the future.

Positive surprises result in major appreciation for out-of-favor stocks, while having minimal impact on favorites.

Negative surprises result in major drops in the prices of favorites, while having virtually no impact on out-of-favor stocks.

Psychology is probably the most important factor in the
market—and the one that is least understood.

*People like exciting stories; they don't
like boring companies. That is the normal
cause of investor overreaction.*

DAVID EINHORN

David Einhorn is an interesting figure in the hedge fund world. He became popular after successfully short selling Allied Capital and Lehman Brothers. With Allied, he went through a nightmare. It started with a speech he gave explaining why he had shorted the stock. In retaliation, Allied managed to get the SEC to investigate Einhorn for supposed market manipulation. Eventually, Einhorn's claims about the company were proven right and he went on to publish a book, *Fooling Some of the People All of the Time*, describing his six-year long battle.

Einhorn was born in Demarest, NJ, in 1968. When he was seven, his family moved back to his mother's hometown of Milwaukee, Wisconsin. In the 1970s, his father helped sell the family business, Adelphi Paints. Though he was a chemist, he enjoyed the process and opened a mergers and acquisitions business out of the basement of their home because he could not get a job on Wall Street.

Einhorn graduated in 1991 from Cornell University with a bachelor's degree in government. During his junior year of college, he interned at the Office of Economic Analysis at the SEC in Washington, and developed a stronger interest in economics. After graduating, he spent two years as an analyst at the investment firm Donaldson, Lufkin and Jenrette, followed by a few years at a hedge fund, Siegler, Collery and Company. The first experience exposed him to the cutthroat and sometimes senselessly hierarchical culture of Wall Street. However, at the next job, he was able to actually learn how to invest and conduct quality research. He would submit weeks' worth of research to his boss who would review the file and come back to Einhorn with a list of insightful questions. In 1996, Einhorn co-founded a long/short value-oriented hedge fund, Greenlight Capital, with just $900,000 in capital. More than half of it came from his parents.

Einhorn is also a pretty good poker player. In 2012, he finished third in a three-day tournament at the World Series of Poker in Las Vegas winning $4.35 million, which he donated to a charitable organization.

One of the things I have observed is that American financial markets have a very low pain threshold.

Market extremes occur when it becomes too expensive in the short term to hold for the long term.

As an investor, my job is to figure out what will happen rather than what should happen.

When people ask me what I do for a living, I generally tell them "I run a hedge fund." The majority give me a strange look, so I quickly add, "I am a money manager." When the strange look persists, as it often does, I correct it to simply, "I'm an investor." Everyone knows what that is.

More leverage means more revenues, which means more compensation. In good times, once they pay out the compensation, overhead, and taxes, only a fraction of the incremental revenues fall to the bottom line for shareholders.

I decide holding gold is better than holding
cash, especially now, where both earn no yield.

There were three basic questions to resolve: First, what are the true economics of the business? Second, how do the economics compare to the reported earnings? Third, how are the interests of the decision makers aligned with the investors?

For years, I had believed that I didn't need to take a view on the market or the economy because I considered myself to be a "bottom up" investor. Having my eyes open to the big picture doesn't mean abandoning stock picking, but it does mean managing the long/short exposure ratio more actively, worrying about what may be brewing in certain industries, and when appropriate, buying some just-in-case insurance for foreseeable macro risks even if they are hard to time.

My grandfather was a gold bug. ... I think he was a few decades too early.

The textbooks presume that easier money will always result
in a stronger economy, but that's a bad assumption.

*One nice thing about gold is that it doesn't
even have quarterly conference calls.*

JEAN-MARIE EVEILLARD

Jean-Marie Eveillard is a French value investor who was born in 1940 in Poitiers. He is officially retired but is still a senior adviser and board trustee to First Eagle Funds. While growing up, his family had no connection to the field of investing. Instead, they worked for the French railroad.

After graduating from the esteemed French business school, École des Hautes Études Commerciales, Eveillard started his career in 1962 as an analyst with Société Générale, one of the oldest banks in France. At that time, security analysis was a new concept in Europe and Eveillard's bosses practiced growth investing, the prevailing philosophy, looking for momentum or glamour stocks instead of investing based on a business's actual value. Bored with growth investing, Eveillard took the opportunity offered by his boss in 1968 to move to Manhattan. Unfortunately, though the environment was different, he was working for the same company and was still required to follow the same philosophy.

However, there was a silver lining for Eveillard, because he learned about value investing after he came to the United States. One day, while riding bikes through Central Park with friends from the Columbia Business School, he expressed his frustration with growth investing. They told him about Benjamin Graham, and intrigued, he immediately went to a bookstore and purchased Graham's books. He considered the experience a life-changing epiphany and tried to convince his boss to let him try value investing. However, it would be 1979 before he would be allowed to do so. In fact, he considered the four years prior to that the most miserable of his career—forced to invest as a growth investor but now a value investor in his heart.

In 1979, he was assigned to manage the SoGen International Fund, a small fund that the bank didn't care about. Several years later, they noticed his superior performance. Eveillard retired in 2004, but was asked to return in 2007 after Charles de Vaulx, his longtime protégé who had taken over the fund, abruptly quit. He was spending his retirement helping to teach a course on value investing at Columbia Business School, attending the opera with his wife, and playing Sudoku, but he agreed to come back for one year.

It's warmer inside the herd. ... It can be very cold outside of it.

There is nothing wrong with making money through simple investment ideas. After all, that's what Warren Buffett has done for years.

Sometimes in life, it's not just about what we buy, but what we don't buy.

There are very few value investors that get involved in shorting because if you are a value investor, you are a long-term investor. If you are a long-term investor, you don't have to worry about market psychology.

We value investors play the game of bridge and the others play poker. The big difference is that there is much less luck in bridge than in poker. I think the secret of success of most value investors is that when times became difficult they stuck to their guns and did not capitulate.

Value investors tend to be patient. If I buy a stock at 15 and four and a half years later it is still at 15 and then in the following six months it goes to 30, the value investor does not say, I wasted my time for four and a half years. He or she says, hey, I doubled my money in five years. I don't care whether it happened smoothly or all of a sudden, I doubled my money in five years.

People say derivatives reduce risk. They don't. They just spread the risk.

[In November 2002.] My attitude is that [Federal Reserve Chairman Alan] Greenspan financed the stock-market bubble, because there can be no bubble unless it's financed by the central bank. Now, he's financed a real estate bubble. The first bubble has burst. If the second, the real estate bubble, bursts, then what does he do? Within the next year or two, either Greenspan will maintain his status, or he will be seen as the worst Fed chief since 1913, when the Fed was created.

When I'm in a good mood, I say Wall Street is nothing but a big promotional machine. When I'm not in a good mood, I say it's a den of thieves.

[In June 2007.] No, we're not looking at homebuilding stocks. I think there was a housing bubble, and as a consequence of the subprime meltdown, I think that housing is not about to recover anytime soon.

Sell-side research is directed towards the 95% or so of professional investors who are not value investors, so their time horizon is usually more along the lines of six to twelve months as opposed to five or more years for us.

Sometimes, there are non-value investors who tell me, well, I would love to do what you do, but if I did it and start lagging, either my boss or my shareholders will fire me. Of course, the answer is you have the wrong boss or wrong shareholders or both!

Peter Lynch was running the Fidelity Magellan fund. Lynch had a superior long-term track record, but he discovered to his dismay that the great majority of shareholders of the Magellan Fund during his management had done much worse than Peter Lynch's record because they usually bought into the fund after Peter Lynch had really hit the ball and then they would leave if for six or nine months if he was doing less well or if the market went down during that period.

You know value investors are bottom-up investors, but I do pay some attention to the top-down.

If a company pays a lower tax rate than its peers, we have to find out why. If there is no valid reason for a lower tax rate, then either the company is cheating the tax authorities or it is overstating its profits.

A lot of investors will not touch a company that is not growing. But the truth is that even if the company is not growing it may be worth a lot. It may have a lot of cash, it may be in an industry which is not growing but may have very few new entrants which can, at times, can be an advantage.

I believe that if a stock is cheap, then investors will eventually recognize its value. It may take three years, five years, or even longer, but the truth is that investing requires patience, and you need a huge amount of it to see good things happen!

I think traders and speculators call it a value trap because their holding period is too short. If the intrinsic value of a stock remains unchanged, then even if its price goes down, it is still a value stock. You can't say that it is a trap just because your holding period is mismatched with the time it takes for the stock to recover. If you have patience, and if your analysis is right, then the market will acknowledge the stock eventually!

As the future is uncertain, my advice is to remember the importance of a margin of safety. As a value investor, you can be bottom-up all you want, but remember to pay some attention to the top-down because government policies are having a severe impact on the health of the world's financial markets.

If you lag in the first year, your clients are okay with it; if you lag again in the second year, they get nervous; and if you lag in the third year, they are gone! Our fund had total assets of around $6 billion in 1997, but by 2000, it was down to $2 billion. I was unhappy, but I constantly reminded myself that I was acting in the best long-term interests of our investors, so I had to do the right thing. When the mania was over, investors came back and praised our discipline. The fund [the First Eagle Global Fund] today has a size of close to $30 billion.

KENNETH L. FISHER

Kenneth L. Fisher is the son of the legendary investor, Philip A. Fisher. He was born in 1950 in San Francisco, California. He attended Humboldt State University to study forestry, but ended up earning a degree in economics in 1972.

After school, he went to work for his father, and in 1979, he founded his own company, Fisher Investments, with just $250. With the help of direct mail, Internet marketing, and radio advertising, he built it into a very successful investment firm that manages $60 billion in assets.

Fisher is the author of more than 10 books including *The Little Book of Market Myths, Beat the Crowd*, and *The Only Three Questions That Still Count*. Fisher is also known for the "Portfolio Strategy" column that he has written for Forbes magazine since 1984. In 2006, he established the Kenneth L. Fisher Chair in Redwood Forest Ecology at Humboldt State University. He is an expert on 19th century logging and has documented more than 35 abandoned logging camps and mill sites in the northern Santa Cruz Mountains.

Wall Street is skeptical of simplicity.

———————✦———————

Investing … is a probabilities game, not a certainties game.

———————✦———————

I often say investing success is two thirds avoiding

mistakes, one third doing something right.

———————✦———————

Professionals are terrible at forecasting bear markets. The media's worse.

I've learned lots of lessons the hard way.

Any stock most folks think of as a "growth stock"

is already too popular to be a good buy.

People forget. So much! So often! So fast!

A stock only has real potential if most folks think it has none at all.

When investors later see that it does have potential, they're

surprised, and the stock gets bid up as its popularity rises.

The past is never predictive. That something happened a certain way

in the past doesn't mean it must happen that way in the future.

Money and markets may never forget, but surely people do. And that will not be different this time, next time, or any time in your life.

———————✣———————

I have great love and respect for market history. As they say, those who don't study history are doomed to repeat it.

———————✣———————

IPOs sell on their sizzle and sex appeal. They're usually classified as high-risk growth stocks. But all stocks that are classified as growth stocks are high risk.

———————✣———————

Folks don't like questioning themselves. If we question, we might discover we're wrong, causing humiliation and pain.

———————✣———————

All investors make mistakes. Even the very best—repeatedly. I make mistakes—lots of them. Some huge ones! I'll make more in the future—I promise. If you think you won't, you're wrong.

———————✣———————

In life, there are roads leading to riches and roads not. There's nothing wrong with ones that don't, but if you travel them you'll go where they take you.

———————✣———————

To build to sell, think like a buyer. To build to last, think like an owner.

Every bull market leads to a bear market.

He [Phil Fisher] was always alone. ... Non-social. Thinking.
Reading. Talking on the phone, yes, but not oriented toward
being with people. A very definite non-people person.

If management owns substantial amounts of stock, they are the stockholder's
partners. They have every incentive to make the shares become more valuable.
They will be particularly protective of the company's balance sheet.

It is best if management's stock ownership is at
least 10 times its combined annual salary.

Companies don't go bankrupt unless they have a lot of debt.

Institutions can't touch most of the stocks available to the little guy. ...
The institutions can invest only in the bigger cap stocks. Why? Liquidity.

There are investment bargains in bankruptcy. The problem is, most folks buy
stocks before the firms go into bankruptcy. The trick is to wait until afterward.

The way most people end up with $1 million in the stock
market is to start out with $2 million. That's right.

PHILIP A. FISHER

Philip A. Fisher was a legendary investor who was born in San Francisco in 1907 and died in 2004. He was the father of Kenneth L. Fisher. He started an investment counseling firm in 1931 and is considered one of the most influential investors of all time. He wrote a very successful book, *Common Stocks and Uncommon Profits*. Fisher graduated from Stanford University with a bachelor's degree in economics and stayed one more year at Stanford's newly created Graduate School of Business Administration. Around that time, the Anglo London and Paris National Bank asked Stanford University to send them a graduate trained in investments. They had none, but sent Fisher who promised to return to Stanford for a second year if it did not work out. As a result, in May 1928, he began working for the bank and was soon made head of the statistical department.

Fisher's foundation in analyzing companies was built during the year he attended graduate school. The group spent one day each week visiting some of the largest companies in the San Francisco Bay area. His professor rejected any company that would agree only to a plant tour. The companies they visited also had to allow the professor and his students to sit with the management for intense questioning. His professor did not own a car, so Fisher offered to drive him so that he could have the privilege of learning what he really thought about the companies while they drove back to school.

Fisher's investment style was to invest in growth companies run by quality managers. His research was much deeper than the research of other investors, and he advocated the use of what he called the "scuttlebutt" approach, which consists of learning about companies by talking to suppliers, customers, and competitors. Warren Buffett read his books, sought him out and learned about the scuttlebutt approach from him.

The successful investor is usually an individual who is inherently interested in business problems.

If the job has been correctly done when a common stock is purchased, the time to sell it is—almost never.

This matter of training oneself not to go with the crowd but to be able to zig when the crowd zags, in my opinion, is one of the most important fundamentals of investment success.

Go to five companies in an industry, ask each of them intelligent questions about the points of strength and weakness of the other four, and nine times out of ten a surprisingly detailed and accurate picture of all five will emerge.

There is a complicating factor that makes the handling of investment mistakes more difficult. This is the ego in each of us.

Most people, particularly if they feel sure there is no danger of their being quoted, like to talk about the field of work in which they are engaged and will talk rather freely about their competitors.

Don't be afraid of buying on a war scare.

Of one thing the investor can be certain: A large company's need to bring in a new chief executive from the outside is a damning sign of something basically wrong with the existing management—no matter how good the surface signs may have been as indicated by the most recent earnings statement.

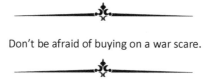

It is often easier to tell what will happen to the price of a stock than how much time will elapse before it happens.

If you know your common stocks equally well, many of the arguments commonly heard for selling the good one sound equally silly.

Investors are not always careful to analyze just what has caused them to buy one stock rather than another. If they did, they might be surprised how often they were influenced by the wording and format of the general comments in a company's annual report to stockholders.

The fact that a stock has or has not risen in the last several years is of no significance whatsoever in determining whether it should be bought now.

The price at which the stock sold four years ago may have little or no real relationship to the price at which it sells today. The company may have developed a host of able new executives, a series of new and highly profitable products, or any number of similar desirable attributes that make the stock intrinsically worth four times as much in relation to the price of other stocks as it was worth four years ago.

In the stock market a good nervous system is even more important than a good head.

The bigger a company is, the harder it is to manage efficiently.

When a stock has been selling too high because of unrealistic expectations, sooner or later a growing number of stockholders grow tired of waiting.

The chief difference between a fool and a wise man is that the wise man learns from his mistakes, while the fool never does.

MARIO GABELLI

Mario Gabelli was born in 1942 in the Bronx to an Italian immigrant couple. His father was a cook at a restaurant and his mother was a homemaker. Gabelli graduated with a bachelor's degree from the business school at Fordham University in 1965 and received his MBA from Columbia University in 1967.

Gabelli first developed an interest in investing as a teenager while caddying at prestigious country clubs where golfers discussed stocks and investing. When attending Columbia Business School, he was taught by Roger Murray, a value investing professor who co-authored the fifth edition of the book *Security Analysis*.

In 1976, he founded Gabelli and Company, a registered broker-dealer. Later, he formed Gabelli Asset Management Company Investors (now GAMCO Investors), a registered investment adviser, to manage money for clients by following Benjamin Graham's investing philosophy.

Gabelli contributed the idea of "private market value" to value investing, which is what an informed buyer would pay for 100 percent of a business. Private market value refers to intrinsic value plus a premium for control—the ability to change the business. Gabelli looks for stocks that are priced below their private market values and that have upcoming catalysts likely to unlock value.

Gabelli has said that he likes to hire "PHDs" who are "poor, hungry, and driven." However, he is known for keeping tight control. A former employee was quoted as saying that many portfolio managers left Gabelli's company because they felt they never got the opportunity to manage money (Vickers).

Businesses don't change in value as quickly as the market.

Sometimes managements forget that they work for shareholders.

Cost of capital always affects a company's values. That's why stocks tend to be valued lower when interest rates rise.

When I started in this business 40 years ago, I spent half my time on research and the other half on things like investment banking. Today I spend half my time on research and the rest hiring analysts.

We believe free cash flow, defined as earnings before interest, taxes, and depreciation (EBITD), or a slight variation, EBITDA, both minus the capital expenditures necessary to grow the business, is the best barometer of a company's value.

When the informed industrialist is evaluating a business for purchase, he
or she is not going to put a lot of weight on stated book value. … What that
informed industrialist wants to know is: How much cash is this business
throwing off today and how much is he going to have to invest in this
business to sustain or grow this stream of cash in the future.

Sophisticated business buyers will look beyond the balance sheet for
hidden assets—valuable land on the books at original cost or an
overfunded pension plan—as well as hidden liabilities, like unfunded
health-care responsibilities or potentially costly environmental problems.

The ideal stock comes with a catalyst—something that will bring the public to it.

We're value-oriented. We're both small-capitalization
and big-cap—we don't care about a company's size.

When things look bleak, there's a great opportunity for everyone.

[On being asked how he found analysts] I told
him we hire only "PHDs" — our shorthand for
Poor, Hungry, and Driven.

We tend to buy what is, not what will be.

MARIKO GORDON

Mariko Gordon founded Daruma Capital Management in 1995. Unlike other investors, she started the firm with zero assets under management.

Gordon has an interesting family history. Her mother's parents left Okinawa, Japan, to work on a plantation in Hawaii. They bought their way out of indentured servitude, bought a farm, and raised pigs. With only an eighth-grade education, her father's father started as a messenger boy in a brokerage firm and worked his way up to partner. He also earned a law degree and a seat on the New York Stock Exchange.

Gordon spent her early years on the French Caribbean island of Guadeloupe, where her parents ran a rental car agency. At the age of 10, they moved to Hawaii where she later became a classmate of Barack Obama in high school. She attended Princeton University, studying comparative literature and graduating in 1983.

She broke into the investment industry in 1986 as an apprentice to a portfolio manager at Manning and Napier in New York. She spent months number-crunching for the company while taking every night course on finance possible in order to fill the information gap left by her humanities education. Later, she joined Royce and Associates, ran by legendary investor Chuck Royce.

Through Daruma Capital Management, she invests in small-cap companies that are undergoing a positive fundamental change, such as a turnaround. She likes to own only a small number of positions in a concentrated portfolio.

Stock picking forces you to eat large doses of humble pie, but it also turns out to be a pretty good diet for the soul.

Simplicity rules. When you're in school, mastering complex stuff is cool. The more complicated it is, the smarter you feel. In investing, it's the opposite: If you don't understand it, it will lose you money. (Even if you do understand it, it can lose you money. But if you don't understand it, it will definitely lose you money).

If it's incomprehensible, it's uninvestable.

No matter how much due diligence you do before you buy a stock, you will never know a company as well as after you've owned it for a while.

A strong stomach is a necessary trait for any professional investor.

In this line of work, you're going to be wrong a lot of time, something that's not always easy to admit. But the key is to be right more often than wrong; to win big and lose small.

School won't turn you into a
world-class cynic—markets can.

You are a blind man groping an elephant. Businesses are complex. They have heaps and heaps of employees, customers, end markets, geographies, regulators, competitors, processes, raw materials, factories, etc. Investors don't really know what's happening inside the elephant—the elephant doesn't always know what's happening inside the elephant. … Today, the elephant is a paintbrush; tomorrow, it's a snake.

Understanding the industry matters. But understanding how a particular company makes money is a more important question in determining its future value.

When it comes to air travel, turbulence is to be expected. If you're not of the same mindset with your investments, you may be in for a bumpy, barfy ride.

Any time a stock doesn't react the
way you think it should to news,
there's an investment opportunity
waiting to be uncovered.

As an investor, you will be destined to mediocrity if you do not continue to grow. Successful investing ... is less about rocket science calculations than it is about avoiding the psychological traps that cognitive dissonance sets for the unwary.

Businesses should not be run with the number one priority
to make their numbers for the next three months.

Once your emotions start driving the process
you're setting yourself up for a bad decision.

*We run concentrated portfolios because,
in our experience, concentration works.
A concentrated portfolio means that
every stock has to earn its keep.*

Being a good investor requires, among other
things, knowing how not to lose money.

BENJAMIN GRAHAM

Benjamin Graham is the "father of value investing." He was born in London in 1894 and died in 1976 in France. He has had a huge impact on many investors including Warren Buffett, who was his student. When he was one year old, he and his family moved to New York City. His father died when he was nine years old, leaving the once financially comfortable family in poverty. Despite the financial struggles, he graduated from Columbia University in 1914 at the age of 20. Afterwards, the English, mathematics, and philosophy departments at Columbia all offered him teaching positions in their respective departments, but he instead went to work on Wall Street as a runner for Newburger, Henderson and Loeb. Within six years, he had become a partner in the firm.

In 1926, he started the "Benjamin Graham Joint Account," and he was joined by Jerome Newman later that same year. The account was later replaced by the Graham-Newman Corporation. In 1928, he started teaching finance at Columbia. Graham and his clients were hit hard by the 1929 stock market crash, but the partnership survived. The only client to make a new investment during the years immediately following the crash was Newman's father-in-law. Because this was near the low point, he was rewarded with a high return. Overall, the experience of the crash taught Graham very valuable lessons, which he laid out in his book.

In 1934, Graham and David Dodd published the classic book, *Security Analysis*, which is still widely read today. In this book, he introduced the concept of "intrinsic value" and the importance of buying stocks for less than what they are really worth. He continued to run the investment partnership until 1956 and had an impressive record, with an average annual rate of return after the management fee of 15.5% from 1945 to 1956. In 1949, he wrote another classic, *The Intelligent Investor*, which is considered the bible of value investing.

There is no sure and easy path to riches in Wall Street or anywhere else.

Investment is most intelligent when it is most businesslike.

You are neither right nor wrong because the crowd disagrees with you. You are right because your data and reasoning are right.

If you are shopping for common stocks, choose them the way you would buy groceries, not the way you would buy perfume.

The one principle that applies to nearly all these so-called "technical approaches" is that one should buy because a stock or the market has gone up and one should sell because it has declined. This is the exact opposite of sound business sense everywhere else, and it is most unlikely that it can lead to lasting success in Wall Street. In our own stock-market experience and observation, extending over 50 years, we have not known a single person who has consistently or lastingly made money by thus "following the market".

There are many ways in which speculation may be unintelligent. Of these, the foremost is 1) speculating when you think you are investing 2) speculating seriously instead of as a pastime, when you lack proper knowledge and skill for it, and 3) risking more money in speculation than you can afford to lose.

The hard part is to adopt it and to stick to it.

Experience teaches that the time to buy stocks is when their price is unduly depressed by temporary adversity. In other words, they should be bought on a bargain basis or not at all.

We are convinced that the average investor cannot deal successfully with price movements by endeavoring to forecast them.

Price fluctuations have only one significant meaning for the true investor. They provide him with an opportunity to buy wisely when prices fall sharply and to sell wisely when they advance a great deal. At other times he will do better if he forgets about the stock market and pays attention to his dividend returns and to the operating results of his companies.

It is undoubtedly better to concentrate on one stock that you know is going to prove highly profitable, rather than dilute your results to a mediocre figure, merely for diversification's sake.

Extremely few companies have been able to show a high rate of uninterrupted growth for long periods of time.

The function of the margin of safety is, in essence, that of rendering unnecessary an accurate estimate of the future.

The margin of safety is always dependent on the price paid.

There are two requirements for success in Wall Street. One, you have to think correctly; and secondly, you have to think independently.

If the share price advances, it is because most investors expect earnings to grow.

The market is not a weighing machine on which the value of each issue is recorded by an exact and impersonal mechanism in accordance with its specific qualities. Rather, should we say the market is a voting machine whereon countless individuals register choices which are the product partly of reason and partly of emotion.

People who habitually purchase common stocks at more than about 20 times their average earnings are likely to lose considerable money in the long run.

The processes by which the securities market arrives at its appraisals are frequently illogical and erroneous. These processes are not automatic or mechanical but psychological, for they go on in the minds of people who buy and sell.

Security prices and yields are not determined by any exact mathematical calculation of the expected risk, but they depend rather upon the popularity of the issue.

JEREMY GRANTHAM

Jeremy Grantham is a British investor who, in 1977, co-founded Grantham, Mayo, van Otterloo and Company (GMO), an investment management firm based in Boston. He was born in 1938 in Hertfordshire, England, and raised by his Quaker grandparents in Doncaster, a coal mining town. He earned his undergraduate degree in economics from the University of Sheffield in the early 1960s and his MBA from Harvard University in 1964.

Unlike many other value investors, Grantham does not ignore the macroeconomic picture. He is considered a "top-down" value investor and is known for calling tops and bottoms in the market. Grantham has studied more than 300 bubbles in history and predicted all the major stock market bubbles of recent decades. He is critical of the policies by the Federal Reserve and believes that the Fed is the reason why the U.S. economy has not been able to recover.

Grantham considers the biggest issue facing society today to be the deterioration of the environment, and in particular, damage to the climate. He and his family have invested in a farm with more than 200 acres in order to conduct comprehensive experiments. The model he wants to study is "mob grazing," or intensive rotational grazing, which is intended to improve the health of the land. He sees farming and forestry as prime investable ideas. Grantham studies energy, metals, water shortages, soil erosion, and the availability of the three macro nutrient fertilizers—nitrogen, potassium, and phosphorus. Based on this research, he predicts how various asset classes will perform.

We will learn an enormous amount in a very short time, quite a bit in the medium term, and absolutely nothing in the long term.

You don't get rewarded for taking risk; you get rewarded for buying cheap assets.

Watching neighbors get rich at the end of a bubble while you sit it out patiently is pure torture. The best way to resist is to do your own simple measurements of value.

If the assets you bought got pushed up in price simply because they were risky, then you are not going to be rewarded for taking a risk; you are going to be punished for it.

People ask what is going to happen next year, and I say I haven't the faintest idea. In general, the short term is unknowable and in an uncertain world, it should be unknowable.

One of the lessons I have learned over the years is that things can get a whole lot more extreme, both up and down, than you ever dreamed of.

Catching a falling knife is never without pain, [but] the prime directive is to buy cheap assets.

Bubbles don't usually stop until sensible investors, value investors, and prudent investors have been hung out to dry and kicked around the block.

The … curse of professional investing is over-management caused by the need to be seen to be busy, to be earning your keep. The individual is far better positioned to wait patiently for the right pitch while paying no regard to what others are doing, which is almost impossible for professionals.

It is easier for an individual to stay cool than it is for a professional who is surrounded by hot news all day long.

There is an enormous pressure in the investment business to deliver good news. Trust me. Good news sells better, stockbrokers thrive on it. Investment houses thrive on it. To go out there in a bubble and talk about badly overpriced markets and downside risks is an invitation to get fired. They simply don`t want to hear it.

Economic theory doesn't work with human beings. We're far too messy. So, economic theory assumes that we're incredibly well informed, that the buyers know just as well as the sellers, which is complete nonsense as everyone knows, and that we're rational and cool and keep a cool head.

The nice thing about bubbles is you don't have to predict them, you just wait and see. And when you see one, you jump.

I am not a professional economist.

JOEL GREENBLATT

Joel Greenblatt is one of the most popular value investors that people like to follow. He was born in 1957 in Great Neck, New York. He earned his bachelor's degree in 1979 and his MBA in 1980 from the Wharton School at the University of Pennsylvania. After earning his MBA, he attended law school for one year to avoid taking a job but was not serious about actually becoming a lawyer. At the end of 1981, he began working for a start-up hedge fund doing risk arbitrage and special situation investing.

In 1985, he started a hedge fund, Gotham Capital, with $7 million from investors. He is now a managing principal and co-chief investment officer of Gotham Asset Management, the successor to Gotham Capital. He is also a professor at the Columbia Business School where he teaches value investing.

Greenblatt co-founded Value Investors Club, a website with exclusive membership where value investors share investment ideas with each other. He is also part owner of Magic Formula Investing, a website that screens for cheap stocks with high returns. He is the author of *You Can Be a Stock Market Genius*, *The Little Book That Beats the Market*, *The Little Book That Still Beats the Market*, and *The Big Secret for the Small Investor*.

The odds of anyone calling you on the phone with good investment advice are about the same as winning Lotto without buying a ticket.

The truth is you can't really tell much of anything just from measuring a stock's past price movements.

Stock market profits can be hiding anywhere, and their hiding places are always changing.

Both spinoffs and merger securities are distributed to investors who were originally investing in something entirely different. Both spinoffs and merger securities are generally unwanted by those investors who receive them. Both spinoffs and merger securities are usually sold without regard to the investment merits. As a result, both spinoffs and merger securities can make you a lot of money.

Companies that are too small for professionals to buy and that are not large enough to generate sufficient commission revenue to justify analyst coverage are more likely to be ignored or misunderstood.

Remember it's the quality of your ideas not the quantity that will result in the big money.

The record of research analysts at major brokerage firms for predicting future earnings or stock prices is quite poor. ... Even institutional clients of reputable investment firms don't get particularly good advice.

Even finding one good opportunity a month is far more than you should need or want.

Companies that achieve a high return on capital are likely to have a special advantage of some kind. That special advantage keeps competitors from destroying the ability to earn above-average profits.

One perennial problem is the overwhelming incentive for analysts to issue "Buy" recommendations. ... It's much easier to generate commissions from new "Buy" recommendations than from recommendations to "Sell".

Your broker, trustworthy or not, has no idea how to invest your money.

If you are going to be a very concentrated investor, you should not use leverage.

The thing you bought goes down and the thing you sold goes up, but I have learned to ignore the pain.

As a general rule, don't buy the common stock of a bankrupt company.

MASON HAWKINS

Mason Hawkins is the founder of Memphis-based Southeastern Asset Management, the investment advisor to Longleaf Partners Funds, which is a suite of mutual funds. Longleaf Partners Funds was created in 1987, and Hawkins is its chairman and CEO. He was born in 1948 in Jacksonville, Florida, and grew up in Thomasville, Georgia. When he was in high school, his father gave him copies of *The Intelligent Investor* by Benjamin Graham, and *Security Analysis* by Graham and David Dodd. In 1970, he earned a bachelor's degree in finance from the University of Florida and, in 1971, an MBA in finance from the University of Georgia.

While he was growing up, Hawkins' family had a lumber business, specializing in the longleaf pine tree, which can live for more than 300 years and is known for its superior quality. The longleaf pine was the perfect symbol for Hawkins' value investing philosophy. In comparison to other types of pine trees, it brings top dollar thanks to its denser, stronger wood, and its ability to resist disease, injury from insects, wind damage, and fire. In the first few years, it appears to grow very little while it establishes a long root, but in the end, it produces the most valuable of southern pine products. On poor sites, after catching up from growing its root, it often outperforms faster-growing pines that have shorter-term economic benefits—just like an undervalued stock eventually outperforming a glamour stock.

Hawkins invests in businesses with good management and strong balance sheets that are trading at low prices. Even though he is a mutual fund manager, he does not shy away from being an activist in order to force change in the companies in which he invests. He also believes in running a concentrated portfolio of no more than 25 stocks.

When you buy businesses at steep discounts from real value, a lot of good things can happen.

We try to hug good investments, not benchmarks.

Valuable growth is the great eraser if you misprice your purchase.

Take advantage of others' fear and greed.

We're looking for two things to line up. The first is that management consists of capable operators focused on generating the most free cash flow possible, and that once they generate that cash flow they redeploy it in a value-generating way.

Chronologically, my dad, Ben Graham, John Templeton, Warren Buffett, and my partner, Staley Cates shaped my investment thinking.

We strive to know as much as we can about our prospective CEO-partners. We want to understand their business acumen and their personal histories.

We sell businesses when they approach intrinsic
value and there's no longer a margin of safety.

*There are three components of an
equity investment's return. One is the
discount to intrinsic value. The second
is the growth in intrinsic value. And
the third is the rapidity at which the
gap between price and value closes.*

CARL ICAHN

Carl Icahn is arguably the most well known activist investor that is alive today. He is the founder and chairman of the board of directors of Icahn Enterprises, a diversified holding company. He was born in 1936, and in 1957, he graduated from Princeton University with a degree in philosophy. Then, he went to medical school but dropped out after two years and joined the army to escape medical school, which he had attended only to appease his mother.

Icahn started his investing career in 1961 as a stockbroker with Dreyfus and Company. Seven years later, he bought a seat on the New York Stock Exchange and founded Icahn and Company, a brokerage firm. While the company started out as a typical Wall Street brokerage firm, in the early 1970s, he shifted the focus to options trading. In 1978, he discovered Tappan, a significantly undervalued appliance maker. He expected a takeover to happen and when none did, he set out to do it himself. This is now known as risk arbitrage—when a group of investors buy shares of an undervalued company, either wait for a takeover or instigate one themselves, and then sell the stock at a satisfying profit. After this experience, he sought other opportunities like it, and in doing so developed a reputation as a corporate raider. In 1985, he acquired Trans World Airlines (TWA) through a hostile takeover, sold its assets to pay the debt he incurred to purchase it, and took it private in 1988. In the end, the company filed for bankruptcy.

Mark Stevens wrote a biography about Icahn titled *King Icahn: The Biography of a Renegade Capitalist*. Icahn has a reputation for being a ruthless bully, although he views himself as nobly fighting to hold inept CEOs accountable and unlock value for shareholders. According to the biography, one mergers and acquisitions chief summed up Icahn in this way, "Carl's dream in life is to have the only fire truck in town. Then when your house is in flames, he can hold you up for every penny you have."

I look at companies as businesses, while Wall Street analysts look for quarterly earnings performance. I buy assets and potentially productivity. Wall Street buys earnings, so they miss a lot of things that I see in certain situations.

My opinion is that, philosophically, I'm doing the right thing in trying to shake up some of these managements. It's a problem in America today that we are not nearly as productive as we should be. That's why we have the balance-of-payments problems. It's like the fall of Rome, when half the population was on the dole.

One of the hidden "assets" in many companies is top management: get rid of them and the value goes up. What's going on in companies these days is absurd. It's like a corporate welfare state. We're supporting managements who produce nothing. No, it's really worse than that. Not only are we paying these drones not to produce, but we're paying them to muck up the works.

I think I'm good at what I do. I think in the takeover business I would say I'm as good as anybody in this area. ... I have a good mind for this type of thinking. It's like a chess game. I was always a good chess player.

Undervalued. Undervalued. Undervalued.

One of our major problems we have in this country is management and the ability to compete. With exceptions we have terrible management in this country.

I can't tell you how bad our boards are, with exceptions of course.

I sit on a lot of boards. I don't have to watch Saturday Night Live anymore, I just sit at the board meetings. And I will tell you that it's a sad commentary that we have an inability to compete. You can blame unions to some extent.

But the real problem is that boards—there's a symbiotic relationship between boards and CEOs today. And as a result, ... there is no way to hold these guys accountable except [when] somebody like myself comes along or some other person who is really willed to challenge them. But you have to go through contortions. There is no corporate democracy.

He's [CEO] a survivor. ... As a survivor, he's not going to ever have a number two guy underneath him who is smarter than him. He doesn't want a guy that can challenge him because God forbid if somebody on the board should meet the number two guy.

He's number two to the CEO. ... Sooner or later, the CEO retires. The CEO puts him there because the CEO realizes this guy's not a challenge because he's a little dumber than the CEO. So now, he becomes the CEO and now he finds his number two guy a little dumber than him. Sooner or later, we're going to be run by morons. By definition. ... And we are not far from that now.

What I look for in these companies are hidden values, values that are not apparent. Analysts look at numbers. They don't see these nonapparent values.

A lot of these companies are undervalued because of poor management. You can replace bad management, right? So, that's one big hidden value there.

IRVING KAHN

Irving Kahn was one of the oldest money managers in the world that was still active in his profession all the way to the end of his life. He died in 2015 at the age of 109. He was born in 1905 in Manhattan.

Kahn graduated from high school in 1923 and attended two years of college. In 1928, he started his career on Wall Street working for a small brokerage firm as a runner on the floor of the New York Stock Exchange. After one week, he wanted out because he thought the people there were crazy, running around and screaming at each other. He went to his boss and was moved to the research department. On evenings and weekends, he worked for another brokerage firm, and in his spare time, he would wander through the building and knock on the door of any office with a light on. One time, he met the head bookkeeper of the company he was working for and had a conversation about the "crazy" market. The bookkeeper had control over the company's profit-and-loss ledgers and showed Kahn Benjamin Graham's account, which stood out because it had almost no losses. Eager to meet him, Kahn sought him out and learned about value investing.

Kahn actually profited from the 1929 crash by shorting a number of shares of Magma Copper—his first trade ever—in June 1929 and doubling his investment when the market crashed in October. Kahn began to sit in on Graham's classes at Columbia Business School and, around 1931, became his teaching assistant. They would ride the subway together to Columbia after trading had closed for the day. Close friends, they went on skiing trips together, and Kahn assisted in the research for Graham and Dodd's *Security Analysis*. Along with Robert Milne, Kahn wrote a biography of Graham's life, *Benjamin Graham, The Father of Financial Analysis*. Kahn was a voracious reader and extremely inquisitive.

Throughout his life, he worked for several different firms including Lehman Brothers. In 1978, he founded Kahn Brothers Group with two of his sons who now run the company. Having lived through the Depression, he was careful with money. He preferred to walk to work or take the city bus, paying the $1 senior citizen fare, instead of taking the $25 car service his company offered to him. Some of his favorite investments were Monsanto and Payless ShoeSource—he bought himself a pair of $49 Payless dress shoes instead of what he considered to be the too-expensive $99 Rockports.

Any market mania comes up against hard reality in the end.

Don't trust quarterly earnings. Verify reports through the source and application statement. Figures can lie and liars can figure.

If you complain that you cannot find opportunities, then that means you either haven't looked hard enough or you haven't read broadly enough.

You don't have to be fully invested all the time. Have patience, keep your standards.

When the Dow Jones Industrial Average dropped 85 percent—from 350 to 50 points between 1929 and 1933—the Great Depression became very real to me.

The Great Depression was like a big storm that sank every ship. It was easy to make money if you had the right approach and knew where to look because some companies were in good shape and had nothing but cash. For example, some export companies were not severely affected by the Depression, but they were beaten down and had net cash per share that was much greater than their stock price. You didn't have to be very smart to find value. All you needed was the right investment model.

Enthusiasts for dollar averaging argued that it made sense to buy more shares when the prices fell in order to "average down" the cost of one's purchases. But the real reason for the popularity of dollar averaging was that it represented a mechanical alternative to market timing based on judgment.

Never buy popular stocks, except maybe in a depression.

History mostly repeats itself, but it's never exact.

I'm a passionate reader. That's why being an investor is the perfect job for me.

If the art of investing were actually easy, or quickly achieved, no one would be in the lower or middle classes.

To be a successful investor, learning is essential.

Security prices are as volatile as ocean waves—they range from calm to stormy.

If a company has great prospects everyone already knows about it. We won't be comfortable paying for good prospects.

[On whether he has a cellular mobile phone at age 106] Yes I do. I don't use it much except to remind myself what my number is.

Do your own homework and don't believe in the newspapers.

We want to grow our money but not necessarily in growth stocks.

SETH KLARMAN

Seth Klarman runs the hedge fund Baupost Group, which is based in Boston. Although he is not known to the general public, he is well known in the value investing community. He is the kind of person that keeps a low profile and rarely grants interviews or speaks publicly. However, he did write a book in 1991 titled *Margin of Safety*. It is now out of print and sells on Amazon.com for $2,000—this is not a typo.

Klarman was born in New York City, and his family moved to Baltimore, Maryland, when he was six. As a child, he loved numbers, from baseball statistics to stock tables in newspapers. He bought his first stock, Johnson and Johnson, at age 10. As a teen, he spent time at Pimlico Race Course and now owns racehorses, giving them names like "Central Banker," "Financial Modeling," and "Read the Footnotes." At Cornell University, he planned to major in mathematics but switched to economics, earning his bachelor's degree in 1979. He discovered value investing during a summer internship at Mutual Shares, and after returning there for a time after graduation, went back to school, earning his MBA from Harvard University in 1982.

Around this time, one of Klarman's professors and three of his friends hired Klarman to manage money for the newly formed

Baupost Group. The name was created from the last names of the four founders—Poorvu, his professor; Stevenson; Baruch; and Auerbach.

In the investment world, money managers want to accumulate as much assets under management as possible. Klarman actually closed his fund to new investors. He understands that the more money he runs, the harder it is to generate excellent investment returns. Unlike many value investors who buy stocks, Klarman prefers bonds. He is extremely risk averse, valuing the preservation of capital over impressive returns.

Value investing requires a great deal of hard work, unusually strict discipline, and a long-term investment horizon. Few are willing and able to devote sufficient time and effort to become value investors, and only a fraction of those have the proper mindset to succeed.

A margin of safety is necessary because valuation is an imprecise art, the future is unpredictable, and investors are human and do make mistakes. It is adherence to the concept of a margin of safety that best distinguishes value investors from all others who are not as concerned about loss.

Once you adopt a value investment strategy, any other investment behavior starts to seem like gambling.

Wall Street research is strongly oriented toward buy rather than sell recommendations. There is more business to be done by issuing an optimistic research report than by writing a pessimistic one.

The focus of most investors differs from that of value investors. Most investors are primarily oriented toward return, how much they can make and pay little attention to risk, how much they can lose.

The problem is that with so much attention being paid to the upside, it is easy to lose sight of the risk.

In addition to the influences of the investment business, money managers (institutional), despite being professionals, frequently fall victim to the same forces that operate on individual investors: the greedy search for quick and easy profits, the comfort of consensus, the fear of falling prices, and all the others. The twin burdens of institutional baggage and human emotion can be difficult to overcome.

The flexibility of institutional investors is frequently limited by a self-imposed requirement to be fully invested at all times. Many institutions interpret their task as stock picking, not market timing; they believe that their clients have made the market timing decision and pay them to fully invest all funds under their management.

The avoidance of loss is the surest way to ensure a profitable outcome.

Speculators are obsessed with predicting — guessing — the direction of stock prices. Every morning on cable television, every afternoon on the stock market report, every weekend in Barron's, every week in dozens of market newsletters, and whenever businesspeople get together.

Sometimes a value investor will review in depth a great many potential investments without finding a single one that is sufficiently attractive. Such persistence is necessary, however, since value is often well hidden.

Value investing is predicated on the efficient market hypothesis being wrong.

Value investing is simple to understand but difficult to implement. Value investors are not super sophisticated analytical wizards who create and apply intricate computer models to find attractive opportunities or assess underlying value. The hard part is discipline, patience and judgment. Investors need discipline to avoid the many unattractive pitches that are thrown, patience to wait for the right pitch, and judgment to know when it is time to swing.

The trick of successful investors is to sell when they want to, not when they have to.

Net-net working capital is defined as net working capital minus all long-term liabilities.

Analysts' recommendations may not produce good results. In part, this is due to the pressure placed on these analysts to recommend frequently rather than wisely.

Yet, high uncertainty is frequently accompanied by low prices. By the time the uncertainty is resolved, prices are likely to have risen.

A simple rule applies: If you don't quickly comprehend what a company is doing, then management probably doesn't either.

When properly implemented, troubled-company investing may entail less risk than traditional investing, yet offer significantly higher returns. When badly done, the results of investing in distressed and bankrupt securities can be disastrous; junior securities, for example, can be completely wiped out.

Some investors place stop-loss orders to sell securities at specific prices, usually marginally below their cost. If prices rise, the orders are not executed. If the prices decline a bit, presumably on the way to a steeper fall, the stop-loss orders are executed. Although this strategy may seem an effective way to limit downside risk, it is, in fact, crazy. Instead of taking advantage of market dips to increase one's holdings, a user of this technique acts as if the market knows the merits of a particular investment better than he or she does.

There is a value gene. You simply get it or not.

EDWARD LAMPERT

Edward Lampert is the founder of ESL Investments. He was born in 1962 in Roslyn, New York, and his grandmother, who was a passive investor, introduced him to investing when he was young. She regularly watched Louis Rukeyser's *Wall Street Week* television program and invested in stocks that paid large dividends. Lampert would sit at her knee as she read stock quotes from the newspaper and they would discuss her investments.

His father, an attorney, died of a heart attack when Lampert was 14 years old. The family had almost no savings and his mother began working at Saks Fifth Avenue as a store clerk. Lampert worked part-time jobs after school and on weekends to help support his mother and sister.

In 1984, he graduated from Yale University with a bachelor's degree in economics. He then went to work for Goldman Sachs where he worked under Robert E. Rubin, who later became the US Treasury Secretary. Lampert's mother was heartbroken when he informed her he had chosen the Goldman Sachs job over his acceptance to both Harvard and Yale law schools, because she didn't know what Goldman Sachs was. Four years later in 1988, Lampert decided to go on his own and start ESL Investments despite his boss's discouragement.

Today, he is one of the best activist hedge fund managers. He is known for writing strongly worded letters demanding board changes and CEO resignations. He likes to say what is on his mind, and was called the "'Kanye West' of Wall Street" by a hedge fund manager interviewed by Vanity Fair (Cohan). As a boy, he used to get in trouble with bullies for having a big mouth, so he hired a school friend to be his bodyguard. In the hedge fund world, he does not need a bodyguard but he does need good lawyers.

He was a classmate of Barack Obama at Columbia University where he earned his economics degree, graduating in 1983. At first, he supported Obama as president, but this is not the case anymore. He is also not afraid to criticize Warren Buffett for preaching one thing and doing something else whether it is in regards to taxes or some other issue.

The only thing I do know is that
from chaos comes opportunity.

I was criticized at my previous jobs for spending a disproportionate amount of time investing and thinking too much like an investor rather than like a salesman, although I was a very good salesman.

The only thing we are 100% confident in is that we are fallible, we don't have all the answers, and we will make some mistakes.

Before you can get into all the nuances of investing and understanding
how to do a due diligence process and question a management team,
you've got to have the nuts and bolts of finance down.

[On hedge fund managing] Make sure you're passionate about investing. I've
seen too many people go into this because they've done the math on the
business model, and have concluded that it's a very lucrative business to be in.
But I've never seen anyone with that approach really make it as an investor.

We must constantly ask ourselves: how much of the bad news is already priced into stocks?

[In March 2009] I have learned a very painful lesson about investing in
less liquid positions. There are times in which the market rewards
investments in less liquid situations with extraordinary returns.

Monetary and fiscal policy can address only issues of liquidity, not solvency.

We love the stocks we own even if we cannot
predict the timing in which they will appreciate.

I think you need to be a little bit of a philosopher to be a good investor.

PETER LYNCH

Peter Lynch is one of the most famous investors. He was born in Newton, Massachusetts, in 1944 and his father became ill with brain cancer when Lynch was seven. When he was 10, his father died, and his mother got a job at Ludlow Manufacturing. To help out, at age 11, Lynch began to work part time as a caddy and continued during high school and college, describing the golf course as "the next best thing to being on the floor of a major exchange" for those who wanted to learn about investing in stocks (Lynch, 49).

The connections he developed on the golf course led him to a scholarship at Boston College and an internship at Fidelity Investments. He studied history, psychology and philosophy and graduated in 1965. When he was a sophomore, he bought his first stock—100 shares of Flying Tiger Airlines for $8 per share. The stock eventually rose to $80 per share. In 1968, he earned his MBA from the Wharton School at the University of Pennsylvania.

After graduation, he returned to Fidelity Investments to work as a research analyst, and this was where he made his name. From 1977 to 1990, when he retired, he ran Fidelity's Magellan Fund, generating a 29.2 percent annual return. He was known for advising people to "buy what you know" and for finding investment ideas by talking to his family and going to shopping malls. He wrote three books with John

Rothchild—*One Up On Wall Street, Beating the Street,* and *Learn to Earn.* Lynch retired in 1990 at the age of 46.

Never invest in any idea you can't illustrate with a crayon.

———————❈———————

All else being equal, invest in the company with the
fewest color photographs in the annual report.

———————❈———————

You don't get hurt by things that you don't own
that go up. It's what you do own that kills you.

———————❈———————

Ask the man you are interviewing about his rivals across the street.
It isn't too significant when the competitors pan a company, but it
is important when they say something nice about it.

A company will rarely go bust in the face of heavy insider buying.

The very best way to make money in a market is in a small growth company
that has been profitable for a couple of years and simply goes on growing.

———————❈———————

I spend about fifteen minutes a year on economic analysis.

———————❈———————

To make money, you must find something that nobody else knows, or
do something that others won't do because they have rigid mindsets.

As a place to invest, I'll take a lousy industry over a great industry any time. Why? Because in a lousy industry, the weak drop out and the survivors get a bigger share of the market.

The key to making money in stocks is not to get scared out of them.

Good information is useless without the willpower.

People invariably feel better after the market gains 600 points and stocks are overvalued, and worse after it drops 600 points and the bargains abound.

The extravagance of any corporate office is directly proportional to management's reluctance to reward the shareholders.

When fund managers receive lots of redemptions (after a correction) it forces them to be sellers when they would like to have been buyers.

For a stock to do better than expected, the company has to be widely underestimated.

I continue to think like an amateur as frequently as possible.

Take the industry that's surrounded with the most doom and gloom, and if the fundamentals are positive, you'll find some big winners. Behind every stock is a company. Find out what it's doing.

Owning stocks is like having children—don't get involved with more than you can handle. The part-time stock picker probably has time to follow 8-12 companies, and to buy and sell shares as conditions warrant. There don't have to be more than 5 companies in the portfolio at any one time.

With small companies, you're better off to wait until they turn a profit before you invest.

Everyone has the brainpower to make money in stocks. Not everyone has the stomach. If you are susceptible to selling everything in a panic, you ought to avoid stocks and stock mutual funds altogether.

Stop listening to professionals!

Dumb money is only dumb when it listens to the smart money.

There seems to be an unwritten rule on Wall Street:

If you don't understand it, then put your life savings into it.

⸻

Be suspicious of companies with growth rates of 50 to 100 percent a year.

⸻

Distrust diversifications, which usually turn out to be diworseifications.

⸻

Invest in simple companies that appear dull, mundane, out

of favor, and haven't caught the fancy of Wall Street.

⸻

Devote at least an hour a week to investment research. Adding up

your dividends and figuring out your gains and losses doesn't count.

⸻

Just because the price goes up doesn't mean you're right.

⸻

Just because the price goes down doesn't mean you're wrong.

When even the analysts are bored, it's time to start buying.

Corporations, like people, change their names for one of two

reasons: either they've gotten married, or they've been involved

in some fiasco that they hope the public will forget.

HOWARD MARKS

Howard Marks is the chairman and co-founder of Oaktree Capital Management, the world's biggest distressed-debt investor. Marks was born in 1946 and raised in Queens, New York. He received his bachelor's degree in finance from the Wharton School at the University of Pennsylvania in 1967 and his MBA from the Booth School of Business at the University of Chicago in 1970. However, before he chose a career in finance and investing, he considered becoming a history professor, architect, or accountant, and, fascinated by Japanese culture, he also completed a minor in Japanese studies.

In the late 1960s, he started his investment career at Citicorp as an equity research analyst. Later, he moved up through the rankings to the director of research and vice president. In 1985, he left Citicorp to join the TCW Group where he invested in distressed debt, high-yield bonds, and convertible securities. In 1995, he and five other partners from TCW ventured out on their own to form Oaktree Capital Management in Los Angeles.

For years, he has been writing memos to Oaktree clients discussing the financial markets and investing. They have become so popular that they have attracted a following that extends beyond the firm's client base and even includes Warren Buffett, who has said that they are the first item in his mail that he opens and reads. They also became the basis for his 2011 book, *The Most Important Thing: Uncommon Sense for the Thoughtful Investor.*

A hugely profitable investment that doesn't begin with discomfort is usually an oxymoron.

———————✖———————

You can't predict. You can prepare.

What the wise man does in the beginning, the fool does in the end.

Believe me, there's nothing better than buying from someone who has to sell regardless of price during a crash. Many of the best buys we've ever made occurred for that reason.

When everyone believes something is risky, their unwillingness to buy usually reduces its price to the point where it's not risky at all. Broadly negative opinion can make it the least risky thing since all optimism has been driven out of its price.

Few things go to zero.

———————✖———————

Those who believe that the pendulum will move in one direction forever—or reside at an extreme forever—eventually will lose huge sums. Those who understand the pendulum's behavior can benefit enormously.

I'd say the necessary condition for the existence of bargains is that perception has to be considerably worse than reality. That means the best opportunities are usually found among the things most others won't do. After all, if everyone feels good about something and is glad to join in, it won't be bargain-priced.

First-level thinking says, "It's a good company; let's buy the stock." Second-level thinking says, "It's a good company, but everyone thinks it's a great company, and it's not. So, the stock's overrated and overpriced, let's sell."

First-level thinking says, "The outlook calls for low growth and rising inflation. Let's dump our stocks." Second-level thinking says, "The outlook stinks, but everyone else is selling in a panic. Buy!"

First-level thinking says, "I think the company's earnings will fall; sell." Second-level thinking says, "I think the company's earnings will fall less than people expect, and the pleasant surprise will lift the stock; buy."

The longer I'm involved in investing, the more impressed I am by the power of the credit cycle. It takes only a small fluctuation in the economy to produce a large fluctuation in the availability of credit, with great impact on asset prices and back on the economy itself.

Why do mistakes occur? Because investing is an action undertaken by human beings, most of whom are at the mercy of their psyches and emotions. Many people possess the intellect needed to analyze data, but far fewer are able to look more deeply into things and withstand the powerful influence of psychology. To say this another way, many people will reach similar cognitive conclusions from their analysis, but what they do with those conclusions varies all over the lot because psychology influences them differently. The biggest investing errors come not from factors that are informational or analytical, but from those that are psychological.

Skepticism is what it takes to look behind a balance sheet, the latest miracle of financial engineering, or the "can't miss" story. … Only a skeptic can separate the things that sound good and are from the things that sound good and aren't. The best investors I know exemplify this trait. It's an absolute necessity.

The absolute best buying opportunities come when asset holders are forced to sell, and in those crises they were present in large numbers. From time to time, holders become forced sellers for reasons like these: 1) the funds they manage experience withdrawals, 2) their portfolio holdings violate investment guidelines such as minimum credit ratings or position maximums, or 3) they receive margin calls because the value of their assets fails to satisfy requirements agreed to in contracts with their lenders.

Look around, and ask yourself: Are investors optimistic or pessimistic? Do the media talking heads say the markets should be piled into or avoided? Are novel investment schemes readily accepted or dismissed out of hand? Are securities offerings and fund openings being treated as opportunities to get rich or possible pitfalls? Has the credit cycle rendered capital readily available or impossible to obtain? Are price/earnings ratios high or low in the context of history, and are yield spreads tight or generous? All of these things are important, and yet none of them entails forecasting. We can make excellent investment decisions on the basis of present observations, with no need to make guesses about the future.

When capital is in oversupply, investors compete for deals by accepting low returns and a slender margin for error.

Leverage magnifies outcomes, but doesn't add value.

Excesses correct.

The air goes out of the balloon much faster than it went in.

The seven scariest words in the world for the thoughtful investor—too much money chasing too few deals.

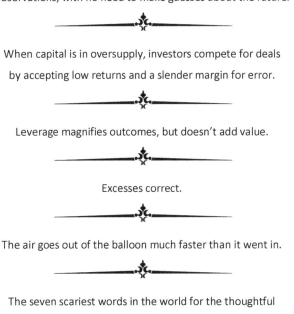

When capital goes where it shouldn't, bad things happen.

MARK MOBIUS

Mark Mobius is considered the "king" of emerging markets. He was the emerging markets fund manager at Franklin Templeton Investments from its inception in 1987 to 2015. Born in 1936 in Hempstead, New York, he received his undergraduate and graduate education from Boston University in fine arts, and communications, respectively, and his Ph.D. in economics and political science from the Massachusetts Institute of Technology. During college, he played in piano bars for fun, using the extra money to supplement his scholarship. He also studied in Japan through an exchange program. Born to a German father and a Puerto Rican mother, Mobius renounced his US citizenship in the mid-1980s to become a German citizen, and stated in his book that it makes traveling easier and safer.

Mobius considers himself a citizen of the world. He attended the Universities of Wisconsin, New Mexico, and Kyoto; studied arts, theater, and psychology; and worked at an advertising agency, a television studio, and various universities as a guest lecturer. He has spent much of his life living on his corporate plane and in hotels all over the world. He has owned apartments in various countries, renting them out because he never stays in one place long enough, and has made more than 2,800 trips to more than 100 different countries, typically spending 200-300 days traveling per year.

A summer job researching consumer data opened his eyes to the fast-growing economic development in various parts of the world. After earning his Ph.D., he moved to Asia in search of a way to connect businesses in the East and West. He landed a job as a research coordinator, conducting thousands of interviews and analyzing more than 100 consumer brands from all over the world. This background provided the foundation for his future career in emerging markets.

Mobius seeks to invest in emerging markets that others are fleeing. He became known for finding stocks that are undervalued in relation to their growth potential and is the author of several books including *The Little Book of Emerging Markets, Passport to Profits, and Foreign Exchange.*

You have to talk to company management, look into their eyes, and determine whether they are reliable.

We're like detectives. We have to discover what's behind the screen of the accounts.

Volatility can be a good thing for investors; be prepared to benefit from it.

Political uncertainty—like any other form of uncertainty—can be your green light to move into a market.

In value investing, money is made after the crash, not before.

When it comes to emerging markets, you cannot rely on the numbers because they cannot be entirely trusted. You have to go out there and start kicking tires.

By the time everyone is trying to get in, we are getting out.

People say emerging markets are dangerous places to invest, but Bernie Madoff operated in the US for years. My belief is that there are good and bad people in every country.

It is important to be a voracious reader. Reading is like your body's muscles; use it or lose it.

When visiting the countries in which I invest I like to talk to working people and people who are actually functioning in the economy.

If the whole world is avoiding a country for exaggerated, short-term reasons, think of shifting it from a hold to a buy.

It is not always possible to predict whether a company is going to be successful or unsuccessful, so it is necessary to diversify.

Frontier markets are generally under-researched. They thus tend to be ignored by the majority of investors.

In one month, approximately 30,000 company research reports are produced in the United States by brokers, banks and other organizations. In Nigeria, it is less than 100.

The people behind the company are just as important as the numbers.

If the management or majority owner doesn't want to meet with you, watch out. They've probably got something to hide.

I'm not too concerned with what's happening to my net asset value. I'm concerned with how many bargains I have in the portfolio.

I love market crashes, panic.

As one of the Rothschilds once said, you must buy when blood is running on the streets—even when it's your own.

CHARLIE MUNGER

Charlie Munger is the investment partner of Warren Buffett and the vice chairman of Berkshire Hathaway. He is also the chairman of the Daily Journal Corporation. Like Buffett, Munger was born in Omaha, Nebraska. However, unlike Buffett, he does not live in Omaha anymore. In 1948, he moved to California, which is where he currently resides.

Munger is very much liked in value investing circles. Thousands of people fly to Omaha every year for the Berkshire Hathaway annual meeting to listen to Buffett and Munger speak. Buffett does more of the talking, but when Munger speaks, the audience knows that something good is going to come out.

Munger is the one who persuaded Buffett to invest in excellent companies with moats instead of just focusing on cheap stocks irrespective of quality—"cigar butt" investing. He was born in 1924, and in high school, he was the captain of the rifle team and part of the Reserve Officer Training Corps (ROTC). After studying mathematics at the University of Michigan for two years, he left to join the army in 1942, choosing the air corps over the infantry because he had grown bored with marching during his ROTC experience. Despite the lack of an undergraduate degree, in 1948, he graduated from Harvard Law School and began practicing in Los Angeles. In the mid-1960s, he left his law career to join Buffett in running Berkshire Hathaway.

Like Warren, I had a considerable passion to get rich, not because I wanted Ferraris—I wanted the independence. I desperately wanted it.

Live within your income and save so that you can invest. Learn what you need to learn.

Do the best you can do. Never tell a lie. If you say you're going to do it, get it done. Nobody cares about an excuse. Leave for the meeting early. Don't be late, but if you are late, don't bother giving people excuses. Just apologize. They're due the apology, but they're not interested in the excuse.

The difference between a good business and a bad business is that good businesses throw up one easy decision after another. The bad businesses throw up painful decisions time after time.

There are huge advantages for an individual to get into a position where you make a few great investments and just sit back—you're paying less to brokers, you're listening to less nonsense.

The game of investing is one of making better predictions about the future than other people. How are you going to do that? One way is to limit your tries to areas of competence. If you try to predict the future of everything, you attempt too much. You're going to fail through lack of specialization.

Frequently, you'll look at a business having fabulous results. And the question is, "How long can this continue?" Well, there's only one way I know to answer that. And that's to think about why the results are occurring now—and then to figure out the forces that could cause those results to stop occurring.

Investors can have 90% of their wealth in a single company, if it is the right company.

Warren Buffett is a learning machine.

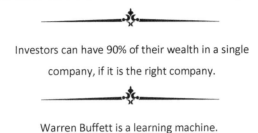

Sit on your ass investing. You're paying less to brokers, you're listening to less nonsense, and if it works, the tax system gives you an extra one, two, or three percentage points per annum.

The big money is not in the buying and selling ... but in the waiting.

We have three baskets for investing: yes, no, and too tough to understand.

We have this investment discipline of waiting for a fat pitch.

The most extreme mistakes in Berkshire's history have been mistakes of omission. We saw it, but didn't act on it. They're huge mistakes—we've lost billions. And we keep on doing it. We're getting better at it. We never get over it.

What is a little surprising is how stupid academia could be. ... There's a lot of silliness in economics.

My idea of shooting fish in a barrel, by the way, is to drain the barrel first.

The one thing that has surprised me all my life is how many people with high IQs do massively stupid things.

There is more dementia about finance than there is about sex.

There is nothing wrong with keeping your head when all about you are losing theirs.

Differing people learn in differing ways. I was put together to learn by reading. If someone is talking to me—it doesn't work as well. With a book, I can learn what I want at a speed that works. It works for my nature.

People attracted to finance today are better suited for snake charming.

Margin of safety means getting more value than you're paying. There are many ways to get value. It's high school algebra; if you can't do this, then don't invest.

When you're trying to determine intrinsic value and margin of safety, there's no one easy method that can simply be mechanically applied by a computer that will make someone who pushes the buttons rich. You have to apply a lot of models. I don't think you can become a great investor rapidly, no more than you can become a bone-tumor pathologist quickly.

Two things matter: if the quality of the business is good enough, it can carry bad management. The reverse isn't true, though. It's very rare for a great manager to take over a bad business, say the textile business, and make it great. You shouldn't look for Warrens.

We recognized early on that very smart people do very dumb things, and we wanted to know why and who, so we could avoid them.

We read a lot. I don't know anyone who's wise who doesn't read a lot. But that's not enough: You have to have a temperament to grab ideas and do sensible things. Most people don't grab the right ideas or don't know what to do with them.

JOHN NEFF

John Neff is considered one of the best mutual fund investors. Before retiring in 1995, he was the manager for Vanguard's Windsor Fund. During his career, he used a value investing approach, but he differed in some aspects. For example, he met face to face with managers of companies he was considering as investments because he wanted to assess their integrity. Also, unlike other value investors, Neff paid attention to the big picture and tried to predict the direction of the economy in order to find individual investments.

Neff was born in Wauseon, Ohio, in 1931 and had a variety of jobs during school and before the start of his investing career, such as working at a jukebox factory, selling cars at a dealership, and working for his father's automobile and industrial equipment supply company. He was in the navy for two years and trained as an aviation electronics technician. He attended the University of Toledo, working 30 hours a week at a shoe store in addition to taking on a full course load, and graduated in 1955 with a bachelor's degree in industrial marketing. He did find time for two courses on finance and investing taught by Sidney Robbins, a disciple of Graham and Dodd who had come from Columbia University. Soon after graduation, Neff began working at National City Bank in Cleveland as an analyst where he researched a broad range of industries. He studied the chemicals industry so thoroughly that an executive at Eastman Kodak, which sold chemicals and related products in addition to cameras and film, remarked that it was obvious that Neff had a chemical engineering degree (Neff, 32).

While continuing to work full time, Neff went to night school to study banking and finance and earned his MBA from Western Reserve University (now Case Western Reserve University) in 1958. In 1963, he switched to Wellington Funds and ran three funds over the course of his career until he retired. He was known for outperforming the market 22 out of 31 years.

You can line up more experts than you can shake a stick at, but none can predict with certainty what investors really want to know: how will the market do tomorrow, or next week, or next year?

Investment success does not require glamour stocks or bull markets.

Conventional wisdom suggests that, for investors, more information these days is a blessing and more competition is a curse. I'd say the opposite is true. Coping with so much information runs the risk of distracting attention from the few variables that really matter.

To us, ugly stocks were often beautiful.

We ... left "greater fool" investing to others.

There is a thin line between being a contrarian and being just plain stubborn.

My whole career, I have argued with the stock market.

Straight lines can throw curves.

Most investors are great at extending straight lines. They have every confidence — or at least a dogged hope — that a hot stock or industry or mutual fund will continue on the same trajectory Expecting more of the same invariably fuels adrenaline markets that culminate in disappointment when enthusiasm wanes.

You don't need stunning growth rates.

No prudent investor puts all the eggs in a single basket. But too much diversification hobbles performance.

Everyone wants to own highly recognized growth stocks. They're ordinarily quite safe, and they seldom embarrass shareholders. That's not a very good case for buying them.

BILL NYGREN

Bill Nygren is a partner and portfolio manager with Harris Associates, an investment firm headquartered in Chicago, Illinois. He manages the firm's Oakmark Select mutual fund. He likes to buy companies that are trading at a discount to their private market values, which refers to what a company would be worth if it were acquired. To determine the private market values, he uses discounted cash flow analysis and considers comparable sale transactions. He has described his investing philosophy by using a version of the 80/20 rule. He believes that when 80 percent of the narrative surrounding a company is focused on a portion of the company that produces only 20 percent of the profits, the stock may be undervalued.

Nygren was born in 1958 and raised in Saint Paul, Minnesota. Like many other investors featured in this book, Nygren fell in love with stocks when he discovered the stock tables in the newspaper across from his beloved baseball box scores. His discovery led him to the library, where he read 30 to 40 books on investing and was captivated by Graham, Buffett and Templeton. He got a job bagging groceries and earned enough to buy 10 shares each of three different stocks.

In 1980, Nygren graduated from the University of Minnesota with a bachelor's degree in accounting, and in 1981, he completed the applied security analysis program at the University of Wisconsin-Madison, graduating with a master's degree in finance. He began his career with Northwestern Mutual Life Insurance Company as an investment analyst and started working for Harris Associates in 1983. Morningstar named Nygren the Domestic Stock Manager of the Year for 2001. Even though he is a value investor, he likes to read about and learn from other successful managers who use different philosophies, such as George Soros or Michael Steinhardt.

Any company that earns an above-average return on assets either has a competitive advantage or is earning above its sustainable rate. It is our job to decide which one it is.

Our basic strategy is to buy a company only when it is trading at 60 percent of its value and to sell them when they achieve 90 percent.

Taking advantage of the values created by emotional investors is the cornerstone of the Oakmark Fund's approach to investing. We try to buy from fearful or bored investors and sell to greedy investors who want excitement.

Every time we look at a business, we try to ascertain how sustainable their results are.

A brand is a very valuable asset, but is usually not on the balance sheet.

The longer it takes for the market to realize the potential of one of our companies, the greater my return is.

A big part of any investor's success or failure in this business is how they manage mistakes. Generally, the sooner you can admit them, the more likely you minimize their impact on your performance.

A lot of my companies achieve my growth estimates through relatively modest top-line growth. A business can use excess cash to improve its balance sheet, buy back shares and shrink its share base, or acquire firms. Any of those can incrementally boost the firm's growth rate. On a per share basis, this can make a relatively mundane business look pretty good.

We are very disciplined quantitatively on the sell side.

Bad news sells more newspapers, and creates more TV news viewers. ... Investors have learned to approach positive news with a healthy dose of skepticism and correctly judge much of what they hear as "too good to be true." But I believe investors have been slow to apply that thinking to the negative, and should also consider the possibility that what they hear is "too bad to be true."

There are two questions that I think we pay more attention to than most investors do: Does forecasted growth require capital investment or will excess cash be generated? And how does management evaluate how to raise needed capital or invest excess capital?

I think we analyze companies much more like Buffett than Graham. ... But unlike Buffett, we do sell stocks when we believe they exceed 90% of value.

If you focus on the not losing part, the upside usually takes care of itself.

MOHNISH PABRAI

Mohnish Pabrai is an Indian-American businessman who became a hedge fund manager. He founded Pabrai Investment Funds in 1999 with $1 million from eight investors. He was born in 1964 in Mumbai, India. In 1983, he moved to the United States to attend Clemson University in South Carolina where he earned a bachelor's degree in computer engineering.

In 1990, while still working at Tellabs, he started TransTech, Inc., an IT consulting and systems integration company, with $100,000 of which $30,000 came from his 401(k) and $70,000 came from credit cards. In October 2000, with revenues at $20 million, he sold it for $6 million.

In 1999, after taking a class on disruptive innovation at Harvard, he founded Digital Disrupters, a business to help established companies either develop an online presence or start new Internet-based counterparts. He acquired several clients, but the startup costs were higher than expected and as a result, the company's cash was quickly depleted. Soon after the dotcom bubble burst in the spring of 2000, all of his financial backers pulled out, forcing him to close the company after only 11 months. A couple of months later, he sold TransTech.

Pabrai is a self-taught value investor and publicly states that he is a copycat of Warren Buffett. He follows Buffett's investment style and structured his investment partnership the same way Buffett structured his in the early days. He has said if it wasn't for Buffett, there would be no Pabrai Funds. He has written two books, *The Dhandho Investor* and *Mosaic*.

It's easier to learn the lessons when you don't take the hits in your own portfolio. But when you take the hits in your own portfolio, those lessons stay with you for a long time.

Heads I win; tails, I don't lose much.

If there wasn't a Warren Buffett, there wouldn't be a Pabrai Funds. ... It is hard for me to overstate the influence Warren Buffett and Charlie Munger have had on my thinking. ... I can never repay my debt to them for selflessly sharing priceless wisdom over the decades.

I have never made a phone call to any management of any of the companies I am an investor in. The way I see it, if they need my help, there is a problem.

There is no such thing as a value trap. There are investing mistakes.

Most of the top-ranked business schools around the world do not understand the fundamentals of margin of safety.

Most of the time, assets trade hands at or above their intrinsic value. The key, however, is to wait patiently for that super-fast pitch down the center.

I was lucky that my father ran a whole bunch of businesses, started, grew, and bankrupted them. Many of these businesses were very highly leveraged. My father was always optimistic and he was maximizing leverage on the business. But they would blow up because there was no stability in them.

What you want is a business that has a deep moat with lots of piranha in it and that's getting deeper by the day. That's a great business.

All investment managers' miseries stem from the inability to sit alone in a room and do nothing.

I think that the way the investment business is set up, it's actually set up the wrong way. The correct way to set it up is to have gentlemen of leisure, who go about their leisurely tasks, and when the world is severely fearful is when they put their leisurely task aside and go to work. That would be the ideal way to set up the investment business.

People think that entrepreneurs take risk. And they get rewarded because they take risk. In reality, entrepreneurs do everything they can to minimize risk. They are not interested in taking risk. They want free lunches and they go after free lunches. The average Chinese company has three sets of [accounting] books. You know, one for the government and one for the owner's wife and one for the owner's mistress. And so the problem you have is you don't know which set of books you're looking at.

There are so many good ideas around.
You don't need to create your own
ideas — you can clone them.

JOHN PAULSON

John Paulson is a hedge fund manager who founded Paulson and Company in 1994. The company specializes in global merger, event arbitrage, and credit strategies. He was born in 1955 in Queens, New York. His father worked at Arthur Andersen and later became the CFO at a public relations firm, and his mother was a child psychologist.

Paulson went to New York University in 1973 and studied creative writing, film production, and philosophy, but became bored with school. Spending part of the following summer with his wealthy uncle in Ecuador rekindled his interest in money. He enjoyed it so much that he stayed for two years but lived on his own, and after a couple of successful business ventures with his father reselling inexpensive children's clothing and parquet flooring, Paulson returned to NYU with renewed enthusiasm in 1976 as his friends were entering their senior year. He felt pressured to catch up and spent 19 months earning the credits he needed and receiving all As. He earned his undergraduate degree in finance from New York University in 1978 and his MBA from Harvard University in 1980.

He started his professional career as a business consultant but eventually went to work on Wall Street for Odyssey Partners and later for Bear Stearns. When he ventured out on his own, he started with $2 million of his own money because he was unable to get any investments from his numerous contacts. By 2003, his fund managed $300 million in assets. At that point, he was still unknown. His popularity skyrocketed after he bet against bonds backed by subprime mortgages in 2006. When the financial crisis of 2008/2009 hit, he personally made nearly $4 billion, becoming an investment celebrity.

No one strategy is correct all the time.

Fear-driven periods in the past have been used
as buying opportunities for savvy investors.

I avoid the media. I'm not sure that actually helps me. Not
participating might make the media more interested.

Sometimes it's difficult to interpret the markets, so we're not going to
play a winning hand every day. Our goal is not to outperform all the
time—that's not possible. We want to outperform over time.

If you're going to come in and then leave, come in and leave; I don't think you'll reap
the benefits of investing with us. Investors that do the best, and have done the best,
are those that stay and compound at above-average rates over the long term.

We view gold as a currency, not a commodity. Its importance as a currency will continue to increase as the major central banks around the world continue to print money.

NELSON PELTZ

Nelson Peltz is an activist investor who founded Trian Fund Management with Peter W. May and Edward P. Garden. He was born in 1942 in Brooklyn, New York. He attended University of Pennsylvania's Wharton School but never graduated. Instead, he dropped out during a school break, intending to accept a job offer to be a ski instructor in Oregon. Needing money for the move, he began driving a delivery truck for A. Peltz and Sons, a frozen food distribution company that had been founded by his grandfather. However, with his father's blessing to try any ideas he had for improving the business, he was hooked, and never made it to Oregon. He helped his father acquire other food distribution businesses and visited them often to assist with product development and marketing plans. Peltz and his brother ended up growing the company from $2 million to $140 million in sales and selling it in 1978. He took the knowledge that he had gained about how to grow a business and started buying up controlling stakes in various companies before turning them around through his activist involvement.

Before making an investment, Peltz and his team write a white paper detailing the company's problems and describing proposed solutions. Peltz believes that while most activist investors focus on financial engineering, which can only take you so far, the real value is in the ability to improve business operations, which he thinks few people possess. One of his successes was the purchase of Snapple in 1997. He and his team transformed the deteriorating brand by developing new products and improving marketing before selling it a few years later for five times their original investment.

Our goal is to work with management, not to replace them.

You can do all your research, but you have to listen to your stomach.

If you find a dollar on the balance sheet, it's worth a dollar. ... But if you find a dollar on the income statement, it's worth ten, fifteen, twenty dollars.

What we live and breathe is on the income statement.

What we try to do is find a business, a good business that is not living up to its potential.

What's on the balance sheet is not what's important, it's the value of the brand.

What business is really about, which is free cash flow.

The good thing about private equity, it that it's up close and personal. The CEO talks to the owner every day, not once a quarter.

Many companies simply aren't living up to their potential and as a result, are selling at low multiples of cash flow.

We invest where we can assemble a real plan to fix the company, and drive a major improvement in performance.

The three key ingredients are: First, companies that sell at reduced multiples and, second, are clearly not living up to their potential, and third, where we can create a plan to substantially enhance their earnings.

The company doesn't know we're an investor, because we've purchased 4.9%, so our stake is still undisclosed. We stay out of the public eye until we have the plan. When we first call management, it's the first time they've heard of us. We tell them by working with us, we believe that by executing our operational plan your earnings and multiple will go up, and the world will be a better place.

When a company gets its first call, they're usually upset. But once we talk to them, we tell them, "We're not here to fire you. We see a great way to make your company more profitable."

We like big dividend payers and investment grade companies. Those companies will not catch cold and die.

You have to ask questions that you intuitively know the answer to.

RICHARD RAINWATER

Richard Rainwater was a billionaire investor who started off his investing career with a losing streak. He was born in 1944 in Fort Worth, Texas, and died in 2015. His father operated a small grocery business and his mother worked at J.C. Penney. At the age of 13, he had a newspaper route but paid other children to actually deliver the papers. In high school, he was involved in drag racing and set a record by winning 26 races in a row. Rainwater graduated in 1966 from the University of Texas, Austin, with a bachelor's degree, majoring in mathematics and minoring in physics.

After earning his MBA from Stanford Business School in 1968, Rainwater worked as a securities trader at Goldman Sachs for two years. While he was still working there, former classmate Sid Bass hired him to manage the Bass family portfolio. Rainwater was quoted as saying that he lost every penny on every deal during the first two years (Hollandsworth). This compelled him to search for a better investment strategy, and he sought advice from Charles Allen, Jr., Warren Buffett, and David Dunn, and studied the investment philosophies of Graham, Dodd, and other successful investors. In the end, he developed his own strategy, timing investments based on business cycles and seeking out sectors of industry with interesting problems. He grew the Bass family wealth from $50 million into $5 billion, earning himself $100 million in the process. In 1986, in search of more control over his investment decisions, he ventured out on his own.

Rainwater was a contrarian and a dealmaker who accurately predicted trends that others missed. He liked to acquire a controlling interest in corporations that were struggling. He then would seek out experts to rehabilitate them while waiting for improvements in the industries in which they operated.

Most people invest and then sit around worrying what the next blowup will be, I do the opposite. I wait for the blowup, then invest.

To succeed ... you have to be obsessed. You need to be engaged: to talk boards into things, to hire the right people, to convince your backers.

When I see a unique and remarkable opportunity, I commit quickly and I invest heavily.

What has always struck me as odd is that if you look at corporations, even corporations that began as family businesses, the way they promote people is based on skill, not bloodlines. But most families continue to make the decisions on who will manage the fortune based on bloodlines. That didn't make sense to me or the Basses.

Once there were five hundred mutual funds and five thousand drilling rigs. Now, it's the reverse.

If it takes spreadsheets and computer programs ... you shouldn't do it. If you can't pencil it out in six lines on the back of an envelope ... forget about it.

> *If you happen to be in the right place at the right time, the capitalist system is a beautiful thing.*

RENE RIVKIN

Rene Rivkin was a very successful Australian stockbroker. He was born in 1944 in Shanghai, China, to Russian-Jewish parents who fled Communism twice—once from Russia in 1917 and once from China to Sydney in 1951. As a small child, he was ill and so skinny that he was put on an all-cream diet for six months. Rivkin studied law at the University of Sydney and graduated in 1969. At the age of 26, he purchased a seat on the Sydney Stock Exchange. He became well known for his flamboyant lifestyle, which he used to brand himself and market his business. He suffered from manic depression and always had a cigar and a set of gold worry beads, which were made for him to help him stop smoking.

Rivkin catered to the corporate stars of the 1980s until the crash of 1987. Around that time, he had surgery to remove a brain tumor, and the Sydney Stock Exchange switched to a computerized trading system, rendering his strengths on the stock trading floor obsolete. After that, he switched to discount stockbroking and catered to the general public.

Rivkin walked the line between what was legal and ethical and what was not. As a young man, his father helped him set up Swiss bank accounts that hid his name. He used them to secretly hold stocks and push the price in whatever direction suited him. He also used a tip sheet he had started in 1997 to intentionally promote stocks he owned, and he hid assets in other people's names. In 2003, he was convicted of insider trading. Once of his biggest scandals was the arson of a printing plant, the only asset of a company that Rivkin had bought from a friend, followed by an insurance payout. The plant was valued at AU$4 million and the insurance payout was AU$53 million. News of the payout sent the share price soaring. Rivkin, several colleagues, and even the insurance company that did the payout were invested in it.

Rivkin's chauffeur and close friend, Gordon Wood, murdered his girlfriend, Caroline Byrne, a 24-year-old model, by hurling her headfirst in a spear-like fashion off of a cliff at a well-known suicide spot because of information she knew regarding Rivkin's activities. In mid-2003, Rivkin was supposed to begin 35 periods of weekend detention but on his first day in jail, he collapsed dramatically and had to be taken out to have surgery for another brain tumor. He managed to avoid returning for seven months. As part of his sentence, his dealers license was taken away and he was banned from providing financial services. In May 2005, he committed suicide. He was 60 years old.

Buy in gloom, sell in boom.

I have never met a rich chartist.

Charting is useful only for one thing as far as I'm concerned, and that's to show you where a stock has been. As for showing you where a stock is going, that is absolute garbage.

I've thrown out the challenge many times. Show me a rich chartist. I can show you plenty of rich fundamentalists. Show me a rich chartist, and then I'll change my mind on charts. I've offered rewards of up to $10,000 for the introduction to a rich chartist. No one has ever claimed that reward. That's got to tell you that chartists are basically in the same field as psychics and fortune tellers.

I have spoken to them and have actually employed them occasionally, just for my amusement. ... The guy didn't want to know anything about fundamentals. He taught me that fundamentals are irrelevant because you can see it all in the charts. He didn't last very long. Be very careful with chartists.

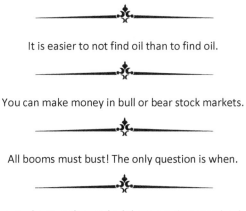

It is easier to not find oil than to find oil.

You can make money in bull or bear stock markets.

All booms must bust! The only question is when.

Anyone who says they picked the exact date is either lying or was lucky. You can never predict the date of a crash, you can only predict that the market is ripe for a crash.

Unless human behavior changes (and it won't), fear, greed and folly will always drive markets.

The pain of losing money is greater than the pleasure of making money.

Missing a stock market winner is not a sin—but losing money is.

I'm against optimism and pessimism in life generally. I believe that there's only one logical position in life, and that's called pragmatism, or realism. I want to see the world, or the stock market, as it is, not as I'd like it to be, or as I'd hate it to be.

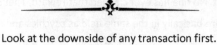

Look at the downside of any transaction first.
If acceptable, then examine the upside.

You can't pay dividends out of losses. No one has invented that yet.

A good company can be overpriced and a bad company can be underpriced.

Almost all my losses have been because I strayed from my investment rules.

Make sure ... that you're not buying absolute garbage.

To make money in the stock market, I believe you have to be entirely passionate (except for long-term investing, which can take care of itself). Be passionate ... live it, breathe it, talk it. You will learn all the time.

When taxi drivers give you tips, it is time to believe the bull market is nearing its end.

If you don't know why you are holding an investment, then sell it.

Never underestimate the importance of patience or luck.

Never spend your profits before you have liquidated the position.

Never buy shares in a company run by people with a shady stock market past.

Be aware that stockbrokers only make money if their clients buy and sell. For many brokers, that is more important than their clients making profits.

The market has a habit of deafening people with information noise. One must cut out the unimportant information and focus on the critical issues.

LARRY ROBBINS

Larry Robbins is a hedge fund manager who founded the New York-based Glenview Capital Management. Glenview is a suburb of Chicago where Robbins learned to play hockey as a young boy. He was born in 1969 in Arlington Heights, Illinois, and in 1992, he graduated with a bachelor's degree in economics and engineering from the Wharton School of Business and Moore School of Engineering at the University of Pennsylvania. He majored in accounting, finance, marketing and systems engineering.

Prior to founding Glenview Capital Management in 2000, he worked for Gleacher and Company, a merger and advisory firm, and Omega Advisors, a hedge fund. His investment strategy is buying growing companies at decent prices. This investment style is called GARP—Growth at a Reasonable Price. Robbins is known for successfully betting on the Affordable Care Act, which he predicted would be signed into law and upheld in court. He invested in hospital companies and health insurers which he believed would benefit from the legislation. This went against the assumption by many on Wall Street that insurers might not fare well.

There are only two things that matter in investing. What are they going to earn, and what multiple are people going to put on that. Let's not make our business any more complicated than this.

We like businesses that are simple to understand and simple to discuss.

You can really prove to yourself whether you know something or not if you can give a five-minute elevator pitch. If you cannot summarize a complex situation in a three- to five-minute discussion, you do not really understand it.

What we're trying to do is complete a jigsaw puzzle, and we're collecting more and more pieces. If I asked you to solve a Wheel of Fortune problem but only gave you two letters, you would have a hard time coming up with the answer. What we're trying to do is uncover as many letters as possible and put together the mosaic.

The stock market was great, because it doesn't know your age. You don't need a Rolodex. You don't need to have contacts or connections. It is a level playing field where 25-year-olds compete with 55-year-olds, and whoever works the hardest and the smartest can do the best job.

If you truly are a sponge, you can learn a lot in many different environments.

If you can lay out the bear case and explain why it is wrong, that should enhance your conviction.

If you own an undervalued equity ... either somebody else will buy that company, the company will buy back its securities at a discount, or the company will do something intelligent by buying another company in a disciplined manner. Going from 0% return on that equity to something like a 10-12% on the equity should be pretty doable.

Basically, we are in the recycling business. There are very few businesses that are public companies today that we haven't looked at.

Even though there are 7,000 public companies in the U.S., when you narrow your search to companies with market cap sizes and type of businesses that make sense to us, we are really dealing with maybe a 1,000 or 1,500 truly investable companies that fit our definition of a good business.

Idea generation is more about idea revisiting today, than it was when we started our fund.

One of the difficult things about being a good fundamental investor is that you want to start out with all of the information, but then you want to synthesize it down to just the important factors. It is always a struggle to not be myopic.

We publish these fifteen-page quarterly letters because it forces us to write down and communicate in a very clear fashion what we think and why we think it. There are a lot of crumpled-up pieces of paper that end up next to the garbage can when we do that. Yet, a lot of times they are a reminder that there are a couple of questions that we still have about an investment that we really should be addressing.

CHARLES M. ROYCE

Charles M. Royce is known as a pioneer of small-cap investing. He is the CEO and portfolio manager of The Royce Funds, a family of mutual funds that specialize in investing in small- and micro-cap companies around the world. He is a bottom-up investor that looks for companies with strong balance sheets, high internal rates of return, and the ability to generate free cash flow. When choosing investments, minimizing risk is more of a priority to him than achieving high returns. He is known for his trademark bow tie.

Royce was born in 1939 and grew up in Maryland. He became interested in stocks when he discovered the Value Line investment surveys at his high school library. He attended Brown University and enrolled in engineering, but switched to economics, graduating in 1961. At Brown, Royce bet on horse racing with his friends. He graduated with an MBA from Columbia Business School in 1963.

After school, he tried to get into Chase Manhattan Bank's training program but was only able to get an analyst position tracking lost dividends. From there, he was able to move up to a junior-level analyst position researching utility stocks. Excited, he started researching anything that interested him until his boss reminded him what his responsibilities were. With little to research in utility stocks, Royce accepted an analyst position at a smaller firm where he got to do a little bit of everything.

In 1968, he became the director of research at another firm where he was responsible for researching what are now called small caps. Around that time, he and a friend bought Pennsylvania Mutual Fund, a shell with no real assets. His friend managed it while Royce continued at his day job. As a result of the economic downturn of the early 1970s, his friend withdrew, Royce's employer went out of business, and Royce was left with the fund. On November 30, 1972, he took it over and lost 40 percent of what was left the first year, and another 40 percent the second year. He convinced the board of directors to let him have once more chance, and when the stock market turned around at the beginning of 1975, the fund began doing well, up 125 percent more than the market.

We are not anti-growth. We are just anti-overpaying for growth.

Essentially, we are interested in three things—a strong balance sheet, a record of success as a business, and the potential for a profitable future.

We spend a disproportionate amount of time looking at the past for clues about the future. We look at return patterns, performance in prior recessions, how managements conducted themselves when they got into trouble. But while a rearview mirror is very important in driving, you can't drive a car with just a rearview mirror. What we're really betting on is the future.

We have an open-door policy on ideas. We don't care how we get them. Our sources are the conventional: the financial press, outside analysts, our internal process.

If you do your work properly in the beginning, there's really no need to reanalyze a company every ten minutes.

Selling, of course, is the toughest part of the equation. I'd love to say that selling is the opposite of buying, but in truth you can develop emotional attachments to the stocks you own.

We are probably too patient with our stocks. We do take a long view, and we tend to buy cheaply, so usually price is not the problem. Opportunity cost is the problem.

I'd like to know who actually came up with that ridiculous phrase risk-on, risk-off.

The truth is that we can't control everything, but we have a very disciplined approach to the stocks we buy. The balance sheet is probably the single most important thing we are looking at.

Customer concentration is a risk factor. ... Maybe the customers put them in business. Maybe the customers need them more than they need the customer. You never know until you peel the onion.

WALTER SCHLOSS

Walter Schloss is an inspirational value investor whose career lasted for five decades. He was born in 1916 in New York City. In 1934, with no college education, he went to work on Wall Street as a runner despite discouragement from his mother's friends who thought that Wall Street would cease to exist by 1940. During that time, his employer paid for him to take night courses taught by Benjamin Graham at the New York Stock Exchange Institute. At the advice of a senior partner at the firm, he read *Security Analysis* by Graham and Dodd the year after it was published.

On December 8, 1941, the day after the Japanese bombed Pearl Harbor, Schloss enlisted in the army and served throughout the war. While he was still in the service, Graham wrote to him and invited him to replace the security analyst he had who was leaving. Schloss began working for Graham in early 1946. In 1955, Graham announced he was going to retire, so Schloss decided to go into business for himself. He gathered $100,000 from 19 partners and instead of serving the enormously wealthy, he focused on those who needed his help.

Schloss never owned a computer and relied on Value Line and annual reports to conduct his research. He avoided talking to members of management because he felt that they tended to paint an overly optimistic picture during difficult times. Schloss preferred more

[At the age of 92] I'm really not in the position to run around the country to meet with management like Peter Lynch used to do. It takes too much out of you. I want to live to be a hundred, so I decided against doing so. I limit myself to looking at the annual report, the balance sheet, looking at the background of the company, seeing that the management owns a lot of the stock in the company and the reputation of the people running it.

Ben [Graham] really loved to teach. He could have made a lot more money if he hadn't been so interested in teaching.

LOU SIMPSON

Lou Simpson is a value investor who used to pick stocks on behalf of Warren Buffett. He worked for the Berkshire Hathaway subsidiary, GEICO. In 2010, he retired and started his own investment company, SQ Advisors, with his wife. Like Buffett, he likes to run a concentrated portfolio consisting of companies that he has researched in great detail. He is known for performing scuttlebutt investment research.

Simpson was the head of investments for GEICO Corporation from 1979 to 2010. In 1993, he became GEICO's president and CEO of capital operations. When Simpson was hired, Berkshire Hathaway owned a large portion of the company, and GEICO's chairman agreed to have the final candidates meet with Buffett. After meeting Simpson, Buffett was sold and told the chairman to stop the search.

Simpson was born in 1936 in Highland Park, Illinois. He enrolled at Northwestern University, intending to study engineering, but transferred to Ohio Wesleyan University the following year and graduated with a bachelor's degree in economics in 1958. He earned his master's degree in economics from Princeton University in 1960. He stayed on at Princeton, working towards his doctorate, but did not finish. Early on in his career, he worked for a firm that had been on a hot streak when he was hired but that took a nosedive a few months later when the market soured. The experience taught him an important lesson and it was around this time that he sought out value investing. Immediately after Simpson was hired as the head of investments for GEICO, he transformed the portfolio by selling bonds and purchasing utility, energy and industrial stocks. He also increased the holdings in food packaging and banking investments. This was a dramatic change because at that time, the typical portfolio of an insurance company comprised mostly bonds and only 10 percent stocks.

Managers who run a profitable business often use excess cash to expand into less profitable endeavors. Repurchase of shares is in many cases a much more advantageous use of surplus resources.

We don't ignore unpopular companies.

In many ways, the stock market is like the weather in that if you don't like the current conditions all you have to do is wait awhile.

I'd say I try to read at least five to eight hours a day.

One of the things I have learned over the years, is how important management is in building or subtracting from value. We will try to see a senior person, and prefer to visit the company at their office, almost like kicking the tires. You can have all the written information in the world, but I think it is important to figure out how senior people in the company think.

The average investor is not properly equipped to be successful.

In general, people are just churning their portfolios. Ben Graham once told me that the way a lot of individuals and institutional investors invest reminded him of people who traded their dirty laundry with each other. They were just trading for the sake of trading, and they didn't really own businesses. Investors are going to make out a whole lot better if their whole emphasis is on owning businesses and having a reasonable time horizon.

Even the world's greatest business is not a good investment, if the price is too high.

GEORGE SOROS

George Soros is one of the most recognizable investors of all time. He is known as "The Man Who Broke the Bank of England" after shorting $10 billion worth of pounds in 1992 and making $1 billion in the process. The British government had failed to prop up the value of the pound and it dropped by 20 percent on September 16, 1992. As a result, the British government was forced to pull the pound from the European Exchange Rate Mechanism.

Soros was born in 1930 in Budapest, Hungary. He survived the Nazi invasion and in 1947, fled communist Hungary for England. In 1952, after working as a railroad porter and busboy to support himself while in school, he graduated from the London School of Economics with a bachelor's degree in economics. He worked at the British investment bank Singer and Friedlander and then sailed to the United States in 1956 to take a job as an arbitrage trader on Wall Street. He later worked as a securities analyst, and in 1969, he founded Soros Fund Management. In 2002, a French court convicted Soros for insider trading because in 1988, he bought and sold shares of Société Générale after receiving information about a planned corporate raid on the bank.

Soros is deeply interested in philosophy, having studied it while at the London School of Economics, and he developed what he calls a general theory of reflexivity, which he says helped him make money as a hedge fund manager and spend it as a philanthropist. He wrote several books including *The Alchemy of Finance*, *Soros on Soros*, and *The Crash of 2008 and What it Means*.

If I had to sum up my practical skills, I would use one word: survival.

I believe that market prices are always wrong in the sense that they present a biased view of the future. But distortion works in both directions: not only do market participants operate with a bias, but their bias can also influence the course of events.

For instance, the stock market is generally believed to anticipate recessions; it would be more correct to say that it can help to precipitate them. Thus, I replace the assertion that markets are always right with two others: 1) markets are always biased in one direction or another; 2) markets can influence the events that they anticipate.

Fundamental analysis seeks to establish how underlying values are reflected in stock prices, whereas the theory of reflexivity shows how stock prices can influence underlying values. One provides a static picture, the other a dynamic one.

Investors operate with limited funds and limited intelligence: they do not need to know everything. As long as they understand something better than others, they have an edge.

Once a trend is established it tends to persist and to run its full course.

The trouble is that not having sold I cannot buy now. All I can do is sit out this round and hope that the situation does not get out of hand.

Financial markets constantly anticipate events, both on the positive and on the negative side, which fail to materialize exactly because they have been anticipated.

It is an old joke that the stock market has predicted seven of the last two recessions.

The United States, in particular, has much to lose if the dollar ceased to be the main international currency. For one thing, the home country of the reserve currency is in an advantageous position to render financial services to the rest of the world. More important, the United States is at present the only country that can borrow unlimited amounts in its own currency. If the dollar were replaced by an international currency, the United States could continue borrowing, but it would be obliged to repay its debt in full. At present, it is within the power of the US government to influence the value of its own indebtedness and it is almost a foregone conclusion that the indebtedness will be worth less when it is repaid than it was at the time when it was incurred.

Markets are often wrong.

People frequently engage in philanthropy because they want to feel good, not because they want to do good.

Good investing is boring.

Survive first and make money afterwards.

Money is closely connected with credit but the role of credit is less well understood than the role of money. This is not surprising because credit is a reflexive phenomenon. Credit is extended against collateral or some other evidence of creditworthiness and the value of the collateral as well as the measurements of creditworthiness are reflexive in character because creditworthiness is in the eye of the creditor. The value of collateral is influenced by the availability of credit. This is particularly true for real estate—a favorite form of collateral. Banks are usually willing to lend against real estate without recourse to the borrower, and the main variable in the value of real estate is the amount the banks are willing to lend against it. Strange as it may seem, the reflexive connection is not recognized in theory and it is often forgotten in practice. Construction is notorious for its boom/bust character and after each bust, bank managers become very cautious and resolve never to become so exposed again. But when they are again awash with liquidity and desperate to put money to work, a new cycle begins.

[Success comes from] preservation of capital and home runs.

Where I do think I excel is in recognizing my mistakes ...
that is the secret to my success.

I am my most severe critic.

I'm a very bad judge of character. I'm a good judge of stocks, and I
have a reasonably good perspective on history. But I am really quite
awful in judging character, and so I've made many mistakes.

I'm fascinated by chaos. That's really how I make my money: understanding the revolutionary process in financial markets.

JOHN TEMPLETON

In 1999, Money magazine called John Templeton "arguably the greatest global stock picker of the century." He was born in 1912 to a poor family in Winchester, Tennessee. He attended Yale University, paying for his tuition by earning scholarships, working three jobs at a time, and winning poker games. In 1934, he graduated with a degree in economics near the top of his class. He also attended Oxford University to earn his master's degree in law, and graduated in 1936.

While growing up, his mother took him, his brother, and some friends on two-month road trips to see as much of the country as they could—museums, historic sites and national parks. After graduating from Oxford, he and a classmate took a seven-month trip through 35 countries, traveling cheaply, even sleeping on wooden beds with wooden "pillows" for 10 cents a night in China. His experience traveling gave him the knowledge and confidence to invest internationally.

In the late 1930s, he started his career on Wall Street working for an investment fund, and in 1940, he opened his own fund management company. Templeton pioneered the use of globally diversified mutual funds, creating some of the largest and most successful international investment funds in the world. He lived frugally and humbly and was a contrarian to the bone, even naming his dog Spotless.

A bargain-hunter, he searched for out-of-favor companies worldwide instead of being tied to one country. In 1968, he moved to the Bahamas, a tax haven, renounced his US citizenship, and became a British and Bahamian citizen. Early on, he had considered becoming a Christian minister or a missionary, and later in life, wrote several books on religion. Queen Elizabeth II knighted him in 1987 in recognition of his charitable works and extensive philanthropy. He died in 2008 at the age of 95.

Bull markets are born in pessimism, grow on skepticism, mature on optimism, and die on euphoria.

People are always asking me where is the outlook good, but that's the wrong question. The right question is: Where is the outlook most miserable?

There's only one reason a share goes to a bargain price: because other people are selling. There is no other reason. To get a bargain price, you've got to look for where the public is most frightened and pessimistic.

If you buy the same securities everyone else is buying, you will have the same results as everyone else.

To buy when others are despondently selling and to sell when others are avidly buying requires the greatest of fortitude and pays the greatest ultimate rewards.

You can't outperform the market if you buy the market.

Chances are if you buy what everyone is buying you
will do so only after it is already overpriced.

When buying stocks, search for bargains among quality stocks. Quality is a company
strongly entrenched as the sales leader in a growing market. Quality is a company
that's the technological leader in a field that depends on technical innovation.
Quality is a strong management team with a proven track record. Quality is a well-
capitalized company that is among the first into a new market. Quality is a well
known trusted brand for a high-profit-margin consumer product.

The stock market and the economy do not always march in lockstep. Bear markets
do not always coincide with recessions, and an overall decline in corporate
earnings does not always cause a simultaneous decline in stock prices.

The only way to avoid mistakes is not to invest—which is the biggest mistake of all.

*An investor who has all the answers
doesn't even understand all the questions.*

Never invest in an initial public offering (IPO) to "save" the
commission. That commission is built into the price of the stock—a
reason why most new stocks decline in value after the offering.

Only one thing is more powerful than learning from experience, and that is not learning from experience.

One principle that I have used throughout my career is to invest at the point of maximum pessimism. That is, the time to be most optimistic is at the point of maximum pessimism.

In almost every activity in life people try to go where the outlook is best. You look for a job in an industry with a good future or build a factory in an area where the prospects are best. However, my contention is that if you are selecting publicly traded investments, you have to do the opposite.

DAVID TEPPER

David Tepper is a hedge fund manager and the founder of Appaloosa Management. He was born in 1957 and when he was four or five years old, he was so good at math—he could do multiplication and complex adding—that his sister, who was in second grade, took him to class for show and tell. Tepper earned his bachelor's degree in economics from the University of Pittsburgh in 1978. He then worked as a credit and securities analyst at Equibank in Pittsburgh before getting his master's degree in industrial administration (comparable to an MBA) from Carnegie Mellon University in 1982.

Before entering Wall Street, he first went to work for a steel company, Republic Steel, in the treasury department. Then, he was recruited by Keystone Mutual Funds in Boston, and later, by Goldman Sachs where he became the head trader of the high-yield or "junk" bonds group, specializing in bankruptcies and special situations investing. He was successful, but didn't quite fit into the "navy-suit, Harvard-type" mold at Goldman Sachs (Pressler). After being passed over for partner too many times, he left in December 1992 and started Appaloosa Management in 1993, focusing on distress investing. He is one of the most successful hedge fund managers in the world.

We keep our cool when others don't. The point is, markets adapt. People adapt. Don't listen to all the crap out there.

We don't really buy high-flyers.
We buy before they get high-flyers.

The media says that hedge funds are the new masters of the universe. ... We're just a bunch of schmucks.

Those who keep their heads while others are panicking do well.

We're value-oriented and performance-based like a lot of funds. But I think what differentiates us is that we're not afraid of the downside of different situations when we've done the analysis. Some other people are very afraid of losing money, which keeps them from making money.

I have too much money to quit. I mean, somebody has to manage my money. I'll also put some money out to other managers so it will be a sensible balance.

Sometimes it's time to make money, sometimes it's time not to lose money. Last year was a time not to lose money; we'll see what this year brings.

[In September 2010] Either the economy's going to start getting better. Or it's not and the Fed's going to come in and then it's going to get better, or at least you're going to get richer in some fashion.

PREM WATSA

Prem Watsa is called the "Canadian Warren Buffett." He is the founder and CEO of Fairfax Financial Holdings in Toronto, Canada. He was born in 1950 in Hyderabad, India, and earned his chemical engineering degree from the Indian Institute of Technology in Chennai. While in college, he played field hockey, table tennis, tennis, and chess. In 1972, with only eight dollars to his name, he moved to London, Ontario, to live with his brother and sister-in-law. There, he attended the University of Western Ontario and earned his MBA, paying his way by selling stationary and air conditioners door to door. After business school, he began working for Confederation Life, an insurance company, and a decade later, inspired by Benjamin Graham and Warren Buffett, he and some colleagues formed the company that would become Fairfax Financial.

Fairfax Financial Holdings is a holding company that is similar to Berkshire Hathaway in that it is engaged in an insurance company that uses the float to invest in undervalued companies. Because he stays out of the public eye, not many people have heard of him. However, in value investing circles, he is well known and respected. He is most known for profiting from the 2008 financial crisis by strategically purchasing credit-default swaps and netting $2 billion.

Buy when you hear the sound of canons.
Sell when you hear the sound of trumpets.

When the music stops, it stops very quickly.

———————✦———————

Trees don't grow to the sky, and markets don't fall to the floor.

———————✦———————

Why do Roman bridges historically last for a long, long time? Why did they last for a long time? The key reason was that the people who designed the bridges had to stand underneath it before the traffic went on. So, they made sure there was a massive margin of safety. And bridges lasted for years and years and years.

———————✦———————

Value investing is all about downside protection—and then trying to make a return on the upside.

———————✦———————

Don't ever think that the [stock] market knows more than you do about the underlying business. That's the biggest mistake you can make.

———————✦———————

As far as a lack of patience in investors, that has always been the case. Investors, even professional investors, are focused on making money in the short term.

———————✦———————

The three most important words in the investing business—Margin of Safety.

MARTIN J. WHITMAN

Martin J. Whitman founded Third Avenue Management, which manages several mutual funds. He is known for being a pioneer in the field of distress investing.

Whitman was born in 1924 in the Bronx to Polish immigrant parents, and served in the navy during World War II. In 1949, he earned his bachelor's degree in business administration from Syracuse University. Following graduation, he spent one year at Princeton in the economics graduate program, but was frustrated by the stringent math requirements. He went to work for a number of investment firms, and nine years later, earned his master's degree in economics from the New School for Social Research (now New School University) through night classes.

In 1974, he started the full-service broker-dealer, M.J. Whitman and Company. Through this company, he focused on bankruptcy and stockholder litigation, and served as an advisor to the US Department of Justice's antitrust division, and the SEC's enforcement division. In 1984, in a hostile takeover, he acquired a small fund and used it to gain control over other companies, mainly through bankruptcy organizations. As a contrarian, he likes to invest in the most out-of-favor sectors and companies in the stock market. He also invests in the debt of troubled companies because he can buy it for 10 or 20 cents on the dollar.

Whitman is the author of four books: *Value Investing: A Balanced Approach*, *The Aggressive Conservative Investor*, *Distress Investing: Principles and Technique*, and *Modern Security Analysis: Understanding Wall Street Fundamentals*. His Distress Investing book is widely read by investors interested in distress and bankruptcy investing.

Diversification is a poor substitute for knowledge.

Biting the bullet is great if it's someone else's teeth.

———————✳———————

A lot of what Wall Street does has nothing to do with the underlying value of a business. We deal in probabilities, not predictions.

———————✳———————

Every investment has something wrong with it.

———————✳———————

In value investing, what you think of underlying factors tends to be more important than what you think other people think most of the time.

———————✳———————

In the financial world, it tends to be misleading to state "There is no free lunch." Rather the more meaningful comment is "Somebody has to pay for lunch."

———————✳———————

What a private buyer will pay to control a company has nothing to do with what the stock sells for on the stock market.

A bargain that stays a bargain isn't a bargain.

If future earnings or cash flows do not create wealth, then
those earnings were fictitious to begin with.

Equity investing always involves trade-offs.

Diversification is only a surrogate, and usually a damn poor surrogate,
for knowledge, control, and price consciousness.

There exist strong Wall Street pressures to have periodic IPO booms.

Much of the world is unknown and unpredictable.
Thus, forecasting will always be an art.

Low profit margins can be a strong reason for purchasing a security if there
are grounds for believing that they will improve. Small improvements in
low profit margins can result in dramatic increases in earnings.

Don't worry about the investments you did not make. Rather, concentrate your
worries on the ones you made, but which you should not have made.

We think all investors should avoid the securities of companies deemed to
have bad managements, regardless of the price of the equity security.

[In distress investing] Chapter 11 bankruptcy is not the
end of the game but the beginning of the game.

Bad managements are, in our view, easier to spot than good managements. Bad managements are marked by self-dealing and/or ineptness in virtually all areas except one—protecting their own positions.

On Wall Street, every speculator is called an investor. This is bad semantics.

DONALD YACKTMAN

Donald Yacktman is one of the world's most successful mutual fund managers. He founded Yacktman Asset Management in 1992. If you are not in value investing circles, it is unlikely that you would have ever heard of him. He is very humble. He answers his own phone and does not hire anyone to handle public relations. He was born in 1941 in Chicago, Illinois, and lived there for many years but relocated to Austin, Texas, to help his daughter rehabilitate from a devastating stroke.

Yacktman graduated from the University of Utah in 1965 with a bachelor's degree in economics. He went to Harvard University for his MBA and graduated in 1967. After grad school, he worked at Continental Bank in Chicago for a short time and, unhappy there, switched to Stein Roe and Farnham to work as a portfolio manager, later becoming a partner. However, despite working there for 14 years, he was never really satisfied because his research-oriented, analytical nature did not match well with the momentum-oriented philosophy of the partner in charge of the firm during that time. He enjoyed success and autonomy at his next job managing the Selected American Shares fund, and his performance the year before he left was so impressive that in 1992, Morningstar named him Portfolio Manager of the Year for 1991. Around that time, however, the management was changing and, despite his superior performance,

Yacktman felt pressured to leave. As a result, he started his own firm, and in doing so, made history by being the first high-profile manager to leave a large company, launch his own fund, and actually succeed at it.

Yacktman's investment philosophy is centered on buying profitable businesses when they disappoint Wall Street. Like other value investors such as Warren Buffett, he does not visit or talk to the management of companies in which he invests. He just lets the numbers do the talking instead of being persuaded by charming CEOs.

Too many people buy stories or trends—they don't buy businesses.

The more logical an investing strategy, the more likely it is to succeed.

———————————

A value trap, to me, is a grubby business not bought cheaply enough.

———————————

I'm not buying for today or tomorrow. This is a marathon.

———————————

I want companies that aren't capital intensive, that earn high rates of return from their tangible assets, and whose managers are good allocators of capital. And then, we wait for them to be battered and out of favor.

———————————

This passion for investing is like fire in the belly. Either you have it or you don't.

Buy big, growing, boring companies when they're beaten down in
price and sell them when prices approach peak valuations.

There are generally two types of investors. You have growth-stock buyers and you
have value buyers. I felt that growth-stock buyers tended to buy better businesses
but paid too much for them. The value investors tended to buy poor-quality lousy
businesses, but because they bought and sold at good prices. They made money,
too. My conclusion: Wasn't there something in between? Something that would
take into account owning good businesses but buying them as undervalued stocks?

If you added up profits of the airline industry every year since Kitty Hawk, the result
would be a negative number. It's a lousy business. The same with hotels.

A manager has five options for the cash that a business generates. First, you can
reinvest it in the business—research and development, marketing, and so forth.
After that, the good, profitable businesses usually have four options: One is to
make acquisitions, which are tricky—like trading baseball players. Another is to
buy back stock, and I like to see a company willing to do this, particularly on price
weakness. Or you can pay down debt—which most very profitable companies
don't have much of anyway—or increase the dividend, which I'm not especially
enamored of because it's double taxation for a tax-paying shareholder.

Slowly you develop your own comfort index in individual businesses that you'd
love to own when the price is right. And when they reach those prices, you
nail them down. The advantage to this is that even if you're wrong about
these businesses, you can almost always at least break even.

There's very low risk in owning large companies. It's hard to kill a company
that is making profits of more than $100 million per year.

If you start with the macro, top-down approach, there are so many decisions to make before you get down to the merits of specific stocks that it dilutes the whole process.

The race is not over. After all, this is a marathon, not a sprint.

> *Technology stocks are like Roman candles. They go up like rockets and flare out. Very few have withstood the test of time.*

A good business has one or more of the following characteristics: 1) earns a high return on assets, 2) has a high market share, 3) has relatively low capital requirements, and 4) has a unique franchise.

Good businesses have managers who know how to use money well. That means being "good capital allocators" and using cash to: 1) put back into the existing business to improve and grow the "crown jewels," 2) make acquisitions that fit with the overall business without overpaying, 3) buy back shares, 4) pay down debt, if the firm is over-leveraged or to reduce debt and improve its credit position, and 5) pay dividends.

The danger of talking to [company] managers is that they tell you what you want to hear, not necessarily what you want to know.

When you have a disruptive period, think of it as a fruit tree that is shaking. Some of the fruit will drop to the ground. You can examine the fruit and see which ones you want.

Our approach won't work every quarter or every year, but over 10 years, it will.

The most important aspect of analyzing management is how well they've invested cash in the past, not what they say they are going to do. Because we typically own companies generating a lot of free cash flow, we're in trouble if management doesn't allocate that cash wisely.

Companies that tend to have high returns usually have low fixed assets and low cyclicality. You will rarely see things like airlines, automobiles, or steel companies or, for that matter, banks in our holdings.

There are three essential ingredients one must have to be a success in this industry. I call them the three I's: Integrity, Intelligence, and Intensity. A person either does or does not have them.

NOTES

Biographical Descriptions

PREFACE

Groz, Marc M. and Forbes LLC. *Forbes Guide to the Markets: Becoming a Savvy Investor*. Hoboken: John Wiley & Sons, Inc., 2009. Print.

Murphy, Brian. "The Rise of an American Institution: The Stock Market." *History Now: The Journal of the Gilder Lehrman Institute*. The Gilder Lehrman Institute of American History, n.d. Web. 6 December 2015.

"New York Stock Exchange." *Encyclopædia Britannica*. Encyclopædia Britannica, Inc., n.d. Web. 6 December 2015.

Oltheten, Elisabeth. "Introduction to Stock Market Investment: The New York Stock Exchange." *Department of Finance*. University of Illinois at Urbana Champaign, 24 September 2013. Web. 6 December 2015.

Terrell, Ellen. "History of the New York Stock Exchange." *The Library of Congress Business Reference Services*. The Library of Congress, October 2012. Web. 6 December 2015.

Waggoner, John. "New York Stock Exchange Ruled 1792-2012." *USA Today*. USA Today, 20 December 2012. Web. 6 December 2015.

BILL ACKMAN

Baker, Liana B. "If At First You Don't Succeed Start Another Fund." *Reuters*. Thomson Reuters, 14 October 2010. Web. 6 August 2015.

"Bill Ackman." *CNBC.com*. CNBC, 6 October 2014. Web. 6 August 2015.

Brooker, Katrina. "Love Him or Hate Him, Ackman Now Runs the World's Top Hedge Fund." *Bloomberg*. Bloomberg L.P., 6 January 2015. Web. 6 August 2015.

Gara, Antoine. "Baby Buffett: Will Bill Ackman Resurrect The Ghost Of Howard Hughes And Build A Corporate Empire?" *Forbes*. Forbes.com, LLC, 6 May 2015. Web. 22 November 2015.

Leonard, Devin. "Bill Ackman's Soft Power." *Bloomberg*. Bloomberg L.P., 10 February 2011. Web. 6 August 2015.

"Our Founders: Karen and Bill Ackman." *Pershing Square Foundation*. The Pershing Square Foundation, n.d. Web. 6 August 2015.

"Pershing Square Holdings, Ltd. Releases Monthly Net Asset Value and Performance Report for December 2014." *Pershing Square Holdings, Ltd.* Pershing Square Capital Management, L.P., 5 January 2015. Web. 23 November 2015.

Sender, Henny, and Gregory Zuckerman. "Gotham Partners Is Snared By a Still-Murky Sand Trap." *The Wall Street Journal*. Dow Jones & Company, Inc., 8 January 2003. Web. 22 November 2015.

Stevenson, Alexandra, and Julie Creswell. "Bill Ackman and His Hedge Fund, Betting Big." *The New York Times*. The New York Times Company, 25 October 2014. Web. 2 December 2015.

"The Pershing Square Foundation awards $17M to Harvard." *Harvard Gazette*. The President and Fellows of Harvard College, 14 April 2014. Web. 23 November 2015.

West, Melanie Grayce. "Giving for Learning—And for Rowing." *The Wall Street Journal*. Dow Jones & Company, Inc., 13 April 2014. Web. 23 November 2015.

LEE AINSLIE

Dobbs, Richard, and Timothy Koller. "Inside a Hedge Fund: An Interview With the Managing Partner of Maverick Capital." *McKinsey on Finance* Spring 2006: 6-11. Web. 6 August 2015.

Foxman, Simone, and Darshini Shah. "Ainslie's Maverick Said to Shop Quant-Driven Stock-Picking Fund." *Bloomberg*. Bloomberg L.P., 26 August 2015. Web. 16 November 2015.

"Investor Insight: Lee Ainslie." *Value Investor Insight* 22 December 2006: 1-9. Web. 16 November 2015.

OneWire. "Lee Ainslie, Founder & Managing Partner—Maverick Capital." Online video clip. *YouTube*. YouTube, 1 October 2013. Web. 6 August 2015.

Strachman, Daniel A. *Julian Robertson: A Tiger in the Land of Bulls and Bears*. Hoboken: John Wiley & Sons, Inc., 2004. Print.

"The World's Billionaires: #1062 Lee Ainslie III." *Forbes*. Forbes.com LLC, 5 March 2008. Web. 6 August 2015.

Weiss, Stephen L. *The Big Win: Learning from the Legends to Become a More Successful Investor*. Hoboken: John Wiley & Sons, Inc., 2012. Print.

BERNARD BARUCH

"About: Our History." *The City College of New York*. The City University of New York, n.d. Web. 28 October 2015.

"Bernard Baruch." *Encyclopædia Britannica*. Encyclopædia Britannica, Inc., n.d. Web. 6 August 2015.

"Bernard Baruch." *Jewish Virtual Library*. American-Israeli Cooperative Enterprise, n.d. Web. 6 August 2015.

"Bernard Baruch: Private Life of a Public Man—The Baruch Family." *The Newman Library of Baruch College: Virtual Archives and Online Exhibits*. The Newman Library of Baruch College, 2008. Web. 29 October 2015.

"Bernard M. Baruch Dead; Funeral Services at Reform Temple Tomorrow." *Jewish Telegraphic Agency*. Jewish Telegraphic Agency, 22 June 1965. Web. 6 August 2015.

"Biographical Sketches: Bernard Baruch." *Hoover & Truman: A Presidential Friendship*. The Harry S. Truman Library and Museum, n.d. Web. 6 August 2015.

Coit, Margaret L. *Mr. Baruch*. 1957. Washington: Beard Books, 2000. Print.

Emerson, W. Eric. *Palmetto Profiles: The South Carolina Encyclopedia Guide to the South Carolina Hall of Fame*. Columbia: University of South Carolina Press, 2013. Print.

Grant, James L. *Bernard M. Baruch: The Adventures of a Wall Street Legend*. 1983. New York: John Wiley & Sons, Inc., 1997. Print.

Kahn, Irving, and Robert D. Milne. *Benjamin Graham: The Father of Financial Analysis*. Charlottesville: The Financial Analysts Research Foundation, 1977. Print.

Kohn, Ray. "Bernard Baruch Dies; Statesman, Financier." *The Free Lance-Star* [Fredericksburg, Virginia] 21 June 1965: 1. Print.

"Mr. Bernard Baruch." The Official Homepage of the United States Army Ordnance Corps & School. *United States Ordnance Corps*, n.d. Web. 6 August 2015. "'

BRUCE BERKOWITZ

"A Real Chelsea Success Story." *Chelsea Record* [Chelsea, Massachusetts] 15 July 2010. Web. 7 August 2015.

"Board of Directors." *Fairholme Funds*. Fairholme Capital Management, LLC, n.d. Web. 7 August 2015.

Cendrowski, Scott. "Bruce Berkowitz: The Megamind of Miami." *Fortune*. Time Inc. Network, 10 December 2010. Web. 7 August 2015.

"Executive Profile: Bruce Robert Berkowitz." *Bloomberg*. Bloomberg L.P., n.d. Web. 7 August 2015.

"'If Not Now, When?'—Bruce Berkowitz." *Graham and Doddsville*. The Heilbrunn Center for Graham & Dodd Investing, Columbia Business School, Winter 2009. Web. 23 November 2015.

Lipton, Joshua. "Bruce Berkowitz Stays in the Sunshine." *Forbes*. Forbes.com, LLC, 14 August 2008. Web. 7 August 2015.

Phillips, Don. "Berkowitz: Ignoring the Crowd Is Painful, But It Works." *Morningstar*. Morningstar, Inc., 9 June 2011. Web. 7 August 2015.

Segal, Julie. "Inside the Mind of Fairholme Capital's Bruce Berkowitz." *Institutional Investor*. Institutional Investor LLC, 11 June 2014. Web. 23 November 2015.

CARSON BLOCK

Ablan, Jennifer, and Sam Forgione. "Exclusive: Short Seller Carson Block Mulls Starting Hedge Fund Management Firm." *Reuters*. Thomson Reuters, 16 October 2014. Web. 7 August 2015.

"About Muddy Waters Research." *Muddy Waters Research*. Muddy Waters Research, n.d. Web. 7 August 2015.

Defotis, Dimitra. "Bearish Bets on Chinese Reverse Mergers." *Barron's*. Dow Jones & Company, Inc., 5 March 2011. Web. 7 August 2015.

Gammeltoft, Nikolaj. "Carson Block Goes Short Unafraid as Chinese Gangsters Chase." *Bloomberg*. Bloomberg L.P., 10 December 2012. Web. 7 August 2015.

McMillan, Alex Frew. "Muddy Waters' Carson Block: 'I'm Proud of the Impact We've Had.'" *CNBC*. CNBC LLC, 18 July 2011. Web. 7 August 2015.

CHARLES BRANDES

Brandes, Charles. *Brandes on Value: The Independent Investor*. New York: McGraw-Hill Professional, 2014. Print.

"Brandes Investment Partners, L.P.: Form ADV Part 2A." *Citi Private Bank ADV Disclosure Documents, Privacy Notices, and ERISA Section 408(b)(2) Disclosure Documents*. Citigroup Inc., 30 June 2015. Web. 7 August 2015.

Carlen, Joe. *The Einstein of Money: The Life and Timeless Financial Wisdom of Benjamin Graham*. Amherst: Prometheus Books, 2012. Print.

"Charles H. Brandes '65, 2015 Alumni Association Award: 'Achievement in a Chosen Profession.'" *Bucknell University Alumni Association Awards*. Bucknell University, n.d., Web. 7 August 2015.

"Corporate Overview: About Charles Brandes." *Brandes Investment Partners*. Brandes Investment Partners, n.d. Web. 7 August 2015.

Erman, Boyd. "Billionaire Investor Sees the Value in Sticking to His Hunch (and Russia)." *The Globe and Mail*. The Globe and Mail Inc., 7 November 2014. Web. 3 November 2015.

"Mr. Charles Brandes." *The Ben Graham Centre for Value Investing: Interviews & Notes*. Ivey Business School, Western University, 22 January 2015. Web. 7 August 2015.

"The 400 Richest Americans: #262 Charles Brandes." *Forbes*. Forbes.com LLC, 17 September 2008. Web. 7 August 2015.

"The World's Billionaires: #1605 Charles Brandes." *Forbes*. Forbes.com LLC, 2015. Web. 7 August 2015.

"Value Investing's Mindset and Pedigree at the Heart of Charles H. Brandes' New Book." *Brandes Investment Partners*. Brandes Investment Partners, 21 November 2014. Web. 7 August 2015.

RON BRIERLEY

Adams, Christopher. "Ron Brierley Resigns from Coats." *The New Zealand Herald*. NZME Publishing Limited, 21 April 2015. Web. 22 October 2015.

Gaynor, Brian. "Brian Gaynor: Brierley Investments Delisting End of an Era." *The New Zealand Herald*. NZME Publishing Limited, 21 June 2014. Web. 7 August 2015.

Hunt, Alison. "Five Things You Should Know About GuocoLeisure." *The Motley Fool*. The Motley Fool Singapore Pte. Ltd., 13 November 2013. Web. 22 October 2015.

Korporaal, Glenda. "Brierley Passes Baton to Weiss at GPG." *The Australian*. Nationwide News Pty Limited, 17 June 2010. Web. 22 October 2015.

Van Den Bergh, Roeland. "Remnants of Empire Fade Away." *BusinessDay*. Fairfax New Zealand Limited, 23 December 2013. Web. 7 August 2015.

Van Dongen, Yvonne. "Sir Ron Brierley: The Old Warrior." *The New Zealand Herald*. NZME Publishing Limited, 3 June 2011. Web. 7 August 2015.

CHRISTOPHER H. BROWNE

"About Tweedy, Browne." *Tweedy, Browne Company LLC*. Tweedy, Browne Fund Inc., n.d. Web. 8 August 2015.

Browne, Christopher H. *The Little Book of Value Investing*. Hoboken: John Wiley & Sons, Inc., 2007. Print.

"Christopher H. Browne Makes $10 Million Gift to the University of Pennsylvania." *PennNews*. The University of Pennsylvania, 28 January 2000. Web. 31 October 2015.

Glassman, James K. "Tweedy, Tried and True: Stick to the Value Stocks." *The Washington Post*. The Washington Post, 3 December 1995. Web. 31 October 2015.

Nicholson, Chris V. "Christopher H. Browne, Value Investor, Dies." *The New York Times*. The New York Times Company, 16 December 2009. Web. 8 August 2015.

"Obituaries: Howard S. Browne; Broker, 89." *The New York Times*. The New York Times Company, 20 January 1994. Web. 31 October 2015.

Shtrakhman, Darina, and Jared McDonald. "U. Trustee Browne Died at 62: Christopher H. Browne Died Sunday of a Heart Attack." *The Daily Pennsylvanian*. The Daily Pennsylvanian, 16 December 2009. Web. 8 August 2015.

Zweig, Jason. "A Career Spent Finding Value." *The Wall Street Journal*. Dow Jones & Company, Inc., 16 December 2009. Web. 8 August 2015.

WARREN BUFFETT

"A Message From Warren E. Buffett." *Berkshire Hathaway, Inc*. Berkshire Hathaway, Inc., n.d. Web. 8 August 2015.

Buhayar, Noah. "Buffett Waits on Fat Pitch as Cash Hoard Tops $50 Billion." *Bloomberg*. Bloomberg L.P., 4 August 2014. Web. 8 August 2015.

Herbst-Bayliss, Svea. "Hedge Fund Manager Loeb Takes Aim at 'Oracle of Omaha' Buffett." *Reuters*. Thomson Reuters, 7 May 2015. Web. 8 August 2015.

Koppenheffer, Dave. "3 Things Warren Buffett Says He Will Never Do." *The Motley Fool*. The Motley Fool, 7 May 2015. Web. 8 August 2015.

JIM CHANOS

Conniff, Richard. "The Fraud Detective." *Yale Alumni Magazine*. Yale Alumni Publications, Inc., September/October 2013. Web. 8 August 2015.

"Faculty Directory: James Chanos, Lecturer in the Practice of Finance." *Yale School of Management*. Yale School of Management, n.d. Web. 8 August 2015.

"James S. Chanos." *The Penn Club of Miami*. Penn Club of Miami, n.d. Web. 8 August 2015.

Sherman, Gabriel. "The Catastrophe Capitalist." *New York Magazine*. New York Media LLC, 7 December 2008. Web. 6 November 2015.

"US vs. China Forum/Debate: About the Speakers." *The Chinese Finance Association*. The Chinese Finance Association, n.d. Web. 8 August 2015.

Weiss, Stephen L. *The Big Win: Learning from the Legends to Become a More Successful Investor*. Hoboken: John Wiley & Sons, Inc., 2012. Print.

PETER CUNDILL

"About Peter Cundill." *The Peter Cundill Foundation*. The Peter Cundill Foundation, n.d. Web. 8 August 2015.

Berman, David. "An Interview with Peter Cundill." *The Globe and Mail*. The Globe and Mail Inc., 27 January 2011. Web. 8 August 2015.

"Deaths: F. Peter Cundill FCA, CFA." *GlobeLife*. The Globe and Mail Inc., 27 January 2011. Web. 8 August 2015.

Fine, Philip. "Obituary: Peter Cundill Found Wealth Where Others Feared to Tread." *The Globe and Mail*. The Globe and Mail Inc., 17 February 2011. Web. 7 November 2015.

Meighen, Michael A. "F. Peter Cundill 1938-2011." *McGill Reporter*. McGill Reporter, 8 February 2011. Web. 7 November 2015.

Risso-Gill, Christopher. *Routines and Orgies: The Life of Peter Cundill, Financial Genius, Philosopher, and Philanthropist*. Montreal: McGill-Queen's University Press, 2014. Print.

Risso-Gill, Christopher. *There's Always Something to Do: The Peter Cundill Investment Approach*. Montreal: McGill-Queen's University Press, 2011. Print.

Roseman, Ellen. "Peter Cundill, a Canadian Investment Star, Dies at 72." *The Star*. Toronto Star Newspapers Ltd., 28 January 2011. Web. 8 August 2015.

"The Aspen Institute Mourns the Loss of Lifetime Trustee Peter Cundill." *The Aspen Institute*. Aspen Institute, n.d. Web. 8 August 2015.

RAY DALIO

Ablan, Jennifer. "Bridgewater's Dalio: Risk-Parity Strategies Not to Blame for Market Turmoil." *Reuters*. Thomson Reuters, 15 September 2015. Web. 5 November 2015.

Bridgewater. "How The Economic Machine Works by Ray Dalio." Online video clip. *YouTube*. YouTube, 22 September 2013. Web. 8 August 2015.

Cassidy, John. "Mastering the Machine: How Ray Dalio Built the World's Richest and Strangest Hedge Fund." *The New Yorker*. Conde Nast, 25 July 2011. Web. 8 August 2015.

Dalio, Ray. "Principles." *Bridgewater*. Ray Dalio, 2011. Web. 8 August 2015.

Freeman, James. "The Soul of a Hedge Fund 'Machine.'" *The Wall Street Journal*. Dow Jones & Company, Inc., 6 June 2014. Web. 5 November 2015.

Gross, Daniel. "Bridgewater May Be the Hottest Hedge Fund for Harvard Grads, but It's Also the Weirdest." *The Daily Beast*. The Daily Beast Company LLC, 7 March 2013. Web. 5 November 2015.

Roose, Kevin. "Pursuing Self-Interest in Harmony With the Laws of the Universe and Contributing to Evolution Is Universally Rewarded." *New York Magazine*. New York Media LLC, 10 April 2011. Web. 8 August 2015.

Teitelbaum, Richard. "Dalio Returns 25% With Diversified Bets as Markets Convulse." *Bloomberg*. Bloomberg L.P., 7 September 2011. Web. 5 November 2015.

"The All Weather Story: How Bridgewater Associates Created the All Weather Investment Strategy, the Foundation of the 'Risk Parity' Movement." *Bridgewater*. Bridgewater Associates, LP, n.d. Web. 5 November 2015.

"The Richest Person in Every State." *Forbes*. Forbes.com LLC, 2015. Web. 8 August 2015.

CHARLES DOW

Befumo, Randy, and Alex Schay. "History of the Dow." *The Motley Fool*. The Motley Fool, n.d. Web. 8 August 2015.

Bishop, George W., Jr. *Charles H. Dow and the Dow Theory*. New York : Appleton-Century-Crofts, Inc., 1960. Rpt. at the Universal Digital Library at Carnegie Mellon University, n.d., Web. 12 November 2015.

Chen, James. *Essentials of Technical Analysis for Financial Markets*. Hoboken: John Wiley & Sons, Inc., 2010. Print.

"Death of Mr. Charles H. Dow." *The Wall Street Journal*. Dow Jones & Company, Inc., 5 December 1902. Web. 12 November 2015.

"Dow Jones Averages: Overview." *S&P Dow Jones Indices*. S&P Dow Jones Indices LLC, a part of McGraw Hill Financial, n.d. Web. 8 August 2015.

"Dow Jones History." *Dow Jones*. Dow Jones & Company, n.d. Web. 8 August 2015.

Evensen, Bruce J. "Dow, Charles Henry." *American National Biography Online*. American Council of Learned Societies, Oxford University Press. October 2008. Web. 12 November 2015.

"Humble Beginnings of the Dow Jones: How a Sterling Farmer Became the Toast of Wall Street. " *Connecticut History*. Connecticut Humanities, n.d. Web. 8 August 2015.

Tofel, Richard J. *Restless Genius: Barney Kilgore, The Wall Street Journal, and the Invention of Modern Journalism*. New York: St. Martin's Press, 2009. Print.

DAVID DREMAN

Dang, Sheila. "Contrarian David Dreman: Why the Low PE Approach Works." *GuruFocus*. GuruFocus.com, LLC, 9 October 2015. Web. 29 October 2015.

Dreman, David. "Be Bullish, Buy Banks." *Forbes*. Forbes.com, LLC, 1 July 2015. Web. 29 October 2015.

Dreman, David. *Contrarian Investment Strategies: The Psychological Edge*. New York: Free Press: A Division of Simon & Schuster, Inc., 2011. Print.

"Dreman Value Management, LLC: ADV Part II, Privacy and Proxy Policies." *Citi Private Bank ADV Disclosure Documents, Privacy Notices, and ERISA Section 408(b)(2) Disclosure Documents.* Citigroup Inc., 25 March 2010. Web. 8 August 2015.

Forbes, Steve. "Steve Forbes Interview: David Dreman, Contrarian Investor, Pt. 1." *Forbes.* Forbes.com, LLC, 30 January 2012. Web. 29 October 2015.

Hale, Nathan. "DWS Dreman High Return Equity Fund: All That Glitters Isn't Gold." *CBS Money Watch.* CBS Interactive Inc., 27 April 2009. Web. 29 October 2015.

"Honorary Degree Recipients: David N. Dreman, LL.D., May 26, 1999." *University of Manitoba: University Governance.* University of Manitoba, n.d. Web. 8 August 2015.

Kimelman, John. "Dreman Still Finds Values This Year." *Barron's.* Dow Jones & Company, Inc., 4 January 2005. Web. 8 August 2015.

Knox, Noelle. "Investing With: David N. Dreman; Kemper-Dreman High Return Equity Fund." *The New York Times.* The New York Times Company, 14 June 1998. Web. 8 August 2015.

Norris, Floyd. "David Dreman, Contrarian Fund Manager, Exits Unbowed." *The New York Times.* The New York Times Company, 9 April 2009. Web. 29 October 2015.

"Overview." *Dreman Value Management, LLC.* Dreman Value Management, LLC, n.d. Web. 8 August 2015.

"Who We Are." *Dreman Value Management, LLC.* Dreman Value Management, LLC, n.d. Web. 8 August 2015.

DAVID EINHORN

Alden, William. "Einhorn Finishes Third in Poker Tournament, With $4.35 Million." *The New York Times.* The New York Times Company, 4 July 2012. Web. 9 August 2015.

"David Einhorn." *Greenlight Re.* Greenlight Re., n.d. Web. 9 August 2015.

Einhorn, David. *Fooling Some of the People All of the Time, A Long Short Story.* Hoboken: John Wiley & Sons, Inc., 2008. Print.

Henning, Peter J. "How Not to Run an S.E.C. Investigation." *The New York Times.* The New York Times Company, 24 March 2010. Web. 9 August 2015.

Shari, Michael. "Andrew Wellington: Writing His Own Songs." *Barron's.* Dow Jones & Company, Inc., 26 April 2014. Web. 14 November 2015.

Teitelbaum, Richard. *The Most Dangerous Trade: How Short Sellers Uncover Fraud, Keep Markets Honest, and Make and Lose Billions.* Hoboken: John Wiley & Sons, Inc., 2015. Print.

"The World's Billionaires: #1006 David Einhorn." *Forbes.* Forbes.com LLC, n.d. Web. 9 August 2015.

Veneziani, Vincent W. *The Greatest Trades of All Time: Top Traders Making Big Profits from the Crash of 1929 to Today.* Hoboken: John Wiley & Sons, Inc., 2011. Print.

Vincent, John Konnayil. *Profiting from Hedge Funds: Winning Strategies for the Little Guy.* Singapore: John Wiley & Sons, Inc., 2015. Print.

Wathen, Jordon. "Allied Capital: 5 Years After its Downfall." *The Motley Fool.* The Motley Fool, 26 March 2015. Web. 9 August 2015.

JEAN-MARIE EVEILLARD

Birger, John. "Eveillard: A Value Maestro's Encore." *Fortune*. Time Inc. Network, 19 June 2007. Web. 9 August 2015.

Chan, Ronald. *The Value Investors: Lessons From the World's Top Fund Managers*. Singapore: John Wiley & Sons Singapore Pte. Ltd., 2012. Print.

Haque, Mohammed Ekramul. "What the Eagle is Eyeing." *Outlook Profit* 19 September 2008: 38-46. Print.

"Jean-Marie Eveillard and Ralph Wanger to Receive Fund Manager Lifetime Achievement Awards at Morningstar Investment Conference." *Morningstar*. Morningstar, 26 June 2003. Web. 9 August 2015.

"Jean-Marie Eveillard." *Financial Sense*. Financial Sense, n.d. Web. 9 August 2015.

"Jean-Marie Eveillard." *First Eagle Investment Management*. First Eagle Investment Management, n.d. Web. 9 August 2015.

"Morningstar Announces Fund Managers of the Year for 2001—In Tough Times, Fund Managers Earn Their Keep." *Morningstar*. Morningstar, 4 January 2002. Web. 9 August 2015.

KENNETH L. FISHER

"About Ken Fisher." *Forbes*. Forbes.com LLC, 16 May 2012. Web. 10 August 2015.

"About the Chair Founder, Kenneth L. Fisher." *Institute for Redwood Ecology*. Institute for Redwood Ecology, Humboldt State University, n.d. Web. 10 August 2015.

"Biography: Personal Interests." *Ken Fisher, Forbes Columnist, Author, Money Manager*. Fisher Investments, n.d. Web. 10 August 2015.

"Form ADV 2A Brochure." *Fisher Investments Private Client Group*. Fisher Investments, 23 March 2015. Web. 10 August 2015.

Frankel, Matthew. "3 Things to Learn from Ken Fisher's Net Worth." *The Motley Fool*. The Motley Fool, 19 June 2015. Web. 10 August 2015.

Hunnicutt, Trevor. "Ken Fisher Plans to Step Down as CEO of Firm." *InvestmentNews*. Crain Communications Inc., 14 April 2015. Web. 10 August 2015.

"Ken Fisher Titles." *Fisher Investments*. Fisher Investments, n.d. Web. 10 August 2015.

"Meet Our Graduates: Kenneth L. Fisher." *Humboldt University Marketing & Communications*. Humboldt University Marketing & Communications, n.d. Web. 10 August 2015.

Reese, John P., and Jack M. Forehand. *The Guru Investor: How to Beat the Market Using History's Best Investment Strategies*. Hoboken: John Wiley & Sons, Inc., 2009. Print.

Thornton, Emily. "Hype from a Financial Guru?" *Bloomberg*. Bloomberg L.P., 9 May 2004. Web. 6 November 2015.

PHILIP A. FISHER

Fisher, Kenneth L. "Philip A. Fisher, 1907-2004." *Forbes*. Forbes.com Inc., 26 April 2004. Web. 10 August 2015.

Fisher, Philip A. *Common Stocks and Uncommon Profits*. Hoboken: John Wiley & Sons, Inc., 1996, 2003. Print.

"Fisher's Investment Philosophy." *Stocks 500*. Morningstar, Inc., n.d. Web. 10 August 2015.

Lavietes, Stuart. "Philip A. Fisher, 96, Is Dead; Wrote Key Investment Book." *The New York Times*. The New York Times Company, 19 April 2004. Web. 10 August 2015.

MARIO GABELLI

"About Us." *GAMCO Investors*. GAMCO Investors, Inc., n.d. Web. 11 August 2015.

Block, Dennis J. and Michael A. Epstein. *The Corporate Counsellor's Deskbook*. New York: Aspen Publishers, Inc., 2004, 2003, 2002, 2001, 1999. Print.

Condon, Christopher. "The Value Fund Manager With the $57 Million Paycheck." *Bloomberg*. Bloomberg L.P., 7 March 2014. Web. 13 August 2015.

GAMCO Investors, Inc. *Annual Report*. Rye, New York: GAMCO Investors, Inc., 2010. *Investor Relations*, n.d., Web. 13 August 2015.

Greenwald, Bruce C.N., et al. *Value Investing: From Graham to Buffett and Beyond*. Hoboken: John Wiley & Sons, Inc., 2001. Print.

Marriage, Madison. "Mario Gabelli: 'Being Born Was the Best Decision I Ever Made.'" *People in Fund Management*. The Financial Times LTD, 1 March 2015. Web. 13 August 2015.

"Part 2A of Form ADV, GAMCO Asset Management, Inc." *Citi Private Bank ADV Disclosure Documents, Privacy Notices, and ERISA Section 408(b)(2) Disclosure Documents*. Citigroup Inc., 31 March 2014. Web. 11 August 2015.

Schleier, Curt. "Fund Manager Mario Gabelli: His Drive Has Taken Him to the Top." *Investors.com*. Investor's Business Daily, Inc., 2 November 2000. Web. 13 August 2015.

Sorkin, Andrew Ross. "'Super Mario' Has a Super Headache." *The New York Times*. The New York Times Company, 25 September 2005. Web. 13 August 2015.

"The World's Billionaires: #1118 Mario Gabelli." *Forbes*. Forbes.com LLC, n.d. Web. 13 August 2015.

"The World's Billionaires: #937 Mario Gabelli." *Forbes*. Forbes.com LLC, 10 March 2010. Web. 13 August 2015.

Vickers, Marcia. "Mario Gabelli's Broken Legacy." *Fortune*. Time Inc. Network, 12 June 2006. Web. 13 August 2015.

MARIKO GORDON

"Making Every Stock Count." Value Investor Insight. 30 December 2009: 1-9. Rpt. at Daruma Capital Management, LLC, n.d. Web. 14 August 2015.

"Our People: Mariko Gordon." Daruma. Daruma Capital Management, LLC, n.d. Web. 14 August 2015.

BENJAMIN GRAHAM

Graham, Benjamin, and David L. Dodd. Foreword. *Security Analysis.* By Warren E. Buffett. 2009. 6th ed. New York: The McGraw Hill Companies, Inc., 2009, 1988, 1962, 1951, 1940, 1934. xi-xii. Print.

Graham, Benjamin, and David L. Dodd. *Security Analysis, The Classic 1934 Edition.* 1st ed. New York: The McGraw Hill Companies, Inc., 1934. Toronto Investment Club. Web. 15 August 2015.

Kahn, Irving, and Robert D. Milne. *Benjamin Graham: The Father of Financial Analysis.* Charlottesville: The Financial Analysts Research Foundation, 1977. Print.

Monks, Robert A. G., and Alexandra Reed Lajoux. *Corporate Valuation for Portfolio Investment: Analyzing Assets, Earnings, Cash Flow, Stock Price, Governance, and Special Situations.* Hoboken: John Wiley & Sons, Inc., 2011. Print.

Reese, John. "Who Was the Great Benjamin Graham, 'Father of Value Investing,' and What Makes Up a Value Strategy?" *Forbes Investing Newsletters.* Forbes Newsletter Group, 5 December 2014. Web. 14 August 2015.

Zweig, Jason. "C250 Celebrates Your Columbians: Benjamin Graham." *Columbia University.* Columbia University, n.d. Web. 15 August 2015.

JEREMY GRANTHAM

"About GMO." *GMO.* GMO LLC, n.d. Web. 15 August 2015.

"Firm History." *GMO.* GMO LLC, n.d. Web. 15 August 2015.

Gandel, Stephen. "Jeremy Grantham: The Fed is Killing the Recovery." *Fortune.* Time Inc. Network, 24 March 2014. Web. 15 August 2015.

Grantham, Jeremy. "GMO's Jeremy Grantham Remains Bullish on Stocks." *Barron's.* Dow Jones & Company, Inc., 1 May 2014. Web. 15 August 2015.

Hickman, Leo. "Jeremy Grantham, Environmental Philanthropist: 'We're Trying to Buy Time for the World to Wake Up.'" *The Guardian.* Guardian News and Media Limited, 12 April 2013. Web. 15 August 2015.

Johnson, Jason. "Mob Grazing Produces Healthy Soil and Livestock." *USDA Natural Resources Conservation Service Iowa.* USDA Natural Resources Conservation Service, n.d. Web. 29 October 2015.

"People: Board of Directors." *GMO.* GMO LLC, n.d. Web. 15 August 2015.

Rotella, Carlo. "Can Jeremy Grantham Profit From Ecological Mayhem?" *The New York Times.* The New York Times Company, 11 August 2011. Web. 15 August 2015.

Stipp, Jason. "Grantham: We're Closing In on Bubble Territory." *Morningstar.* Morningstar, Inc., 24 June 2015. Web. 15 August 2015.

Summers, Nick. "GMO's Jeremy Grantham on Climate Change and Investable Ideas." *Bloomberg.* Bloomberg L.P., 8 August 2013. Web. 29 October 2015.

Wathen, Jordan. "Jeremy Grantham: 3 Insights From a Top-Down Value Investor." *The Motley Fool.* The Motley Fool, 2 June 2015. Web. 15 August 2015.

JOEL GREENBLATT

"About VIC." *Value Investors Club*. ValueInvestorsClub.com, n.d. Web. 15 August 2015.

"Answers from Joel Greenblatt are Here!" *GuruFocus*. GuruFocus.com, LLC, 30 June 2009. Web. 14 November 2015.

"Form ADV Part 2B: Gotham Asset Management, LLC." *Lexis Securities Mosaic*. LexisNexis., 27 July 2011. Web. 9 November 2015.

"Frequently Asked Questions." *Magic Formula Investing*. Magic Formula Investing, n.d. Web. 15 August 2015.

"Interact With Top Investors." *Value Investors Club*. ValueInvestorsClub.com, n.d. Web. 15 August 2015.

"Joel Greenblatt." *Gotham Funds*. Gotham Asset Management, LLC, n.d. Web. 15 August 2015.

Kolker, Robert. "How Is a Hedge Fund Like a School?" *New York Magazine*. New York Media LLC, 20 February 2006. Web. 14 November 2015.

MASON HAWKINS

"About Us." *Longleaf Partners Funds*. Southeastern Asset Management, Inc., n.d. Web. 16 August 2015.

Forgione, Sam. "Chesapeake Up Against Low-Key Activist Mason Hawkins." *Reuters*. Thomson Reuters, 11 May 2012. Web. 16 August 2015.

Gould, Carole. "Manager's Profile." *The New York Times*. The New York Times Company, 1 May 1994. Web. 16 August 2015.

"Longleaf Pine." *National Wildlife Federation*. National Wildlife Federation, n.d. Web. 16 August 2015.

"O. Mason Hawkins." *Tiger 21*. Tiger 21, LLC, n.d. Web. 16 August 2015.

"Our Investment Team." *Longleaf Partners Funds*. Southeastern Asset Management, Inc., n.d. Web. 16 August 2015.

"'Parsimony is Extremely Profitable'—Mason Hawkins." *Graham and Doddsville*. The Heilbrunn Center for Graham & Dodd Investing, Columbia Business School, Winter 2010. Web. 30 November 2015.

"The Economics of Longleaf Pine Management." *Longleaf Leaflet*. The North Carolina Forest Service, March 2011. Web. 16 August 2015.

"The Economics of Longleaf Pine Management." *The Longleaf Alliance*. America's Longleaf, n.d. Web. 16 August 2015.

Zweig, Jason. "The Best Mutual Fund Family in America." *CNN Money*. Cable News Network, A Time Warner Company, 1 August 1998. Web. 16 August 2015.

CARL ICAHN

Carey, Charles W., Jr. *American Inventors, Entrepreneurs, and Business Visionaries*. New York: Facts on File, Inc., 2002. Print.

"Corporate Governance: Board of Directors." *Icahn Enterprises L.P.* Icahn Enterprises, n.d. Web. 17 November 2015.

Hartocollis, Anemona. "$200 Million Gift, and a New Name, for Mt. Sinai Medical School." *The New York Times.* The New York Times Company, 14 November 2012. Web. 10 August 2015.

Solomon, Jesse. "Shrewd Investor Carl Icahn is Killing It." *CNN Money.* Cable News Network, 30 September 2014. Web. 10 August 2015.

Stevens, Mark. *King Icahn: The Biography of a Renegade Capitalist.* New York: Penguin Group, 1993, 2014. Print.

"The First 25: Rebels, Icons and Leaders, 17. Carl Icahn." *CNBC.* CNBC LLC, 29 April 2014. Web. 10 August 2015.

"Welcome." *Icahn Enterprises L.P.* Icahn Enterprises, n.d. Web. 17 November 2015.

IRVING KAHN

Bary, Andrew. "Living Legend." *Barron's.* Dow Jones & Company, Inc., 19 December 2005. Web. 3 September 2015.

Chan, Ronald. *The Value Investors: Lessons From the World's Top Fund Managers.* Singapore: John Wiley & Sons Singapore Pte. Ltd., 2012. Print.

Kahn, Irving, and Robert D. Milne. *Benjamin Graham: The Father of Financial Analysis.* Charlottesville: The Financial Analysts Research Foundation, 1977. Print.

"Paid Death Notices: Irving Kahn." *The New York Times.* The New York Times Company, 27 February 2015. Web. 3 September 2015.

Roberts, Sam. "Irving Kahn, Oldest Wall Street Investor, Dies at 109." *The New York Times.* The New York Times Company, 26 February 2015. Web. 2 September 2015.

Zweig, Jason. "Investor Irving Kahn, Disciple of Benjamin Graham, Dies at 109." *The Wall Street Journal.* Dow Jones & Company, Inc., 26 February 2015. Web. 2 September 2015.

Zweig, Jason. "The 107-Year-Old Stock Picker." *The Wall Street Journal.* Dow Jones & Company, Inc., 21 December 2012. Web. 2 September 2015.

SETH KLARMAN

"Alumni Stories: Seth Klarman, MBA 1982." *Harvard Business School.* President & Fellows of Harvard College, n.d. Web. 16 August 2015.

Ember, Sydney. "A Central Banker of a Different Color." *The New York Times.* The New York Times Company, 5 May 2014. Web. 16 August 2015.

"Seth Klarman: The Oracle of Boston." *The Economist.* The Economist Newspaper Limited. 7 July 2012. Web. 16 August 2015.

Taub, Stephen. "The Value of Seth Klarman." *Institutional Investor's Alpha.* Euromoney Institutional Investor PLC, 1 June 2010. Web. 16 August 2015.

"The World's Billionaires: #1250 Seth Klarman." *Forbes.* Forbes.com LLC, n.d. Web. 16 August 2015.

EDWARD LAMPERT

Allison, Kevin. "Disappointment in Latest Sears Plan to Raise Cash." *The New York Times*. The New York Times Company, 3 October 2014. Web. 30 November 2015.

Atlas, Riva D. "'Goldman Sachs' on a Resume Gives Continuing Rewards." *The New York Times*. The New York Times Company, 3 February 2005. Web. 16 August 2015.

Berner, Robert, and Susann Rutledge. "The Next Warren Buffett?" *Bloomberg*. Bloomberg L.P., 21 November 2004. Web. 16 August 2015.

"Edward S. Lampert." *Encyclopædia Britannica*. Encyclopædia Britannica, Inc., n.d. Web. 16 August 2015.

Egan, Matt. "Sears to Make First Profit Since 2012. But Don't Be Fooled." *CNN Money*. Cable News Network, A Time Warner Company, 3 August 2015. Web. 16 August 2015.

Sellers, Patricia. "Eddie Lampert: The Best Investor of His Generation." *Fortune: Investor's Guide 2006*. Time Inc. Network, 6 February 2006. Web. 16 August 2015.

DANIEL LOEB

Ahuja, Maneet. *The Alpha Masters: Unlocking the Genius of the World's Top Hedge Funds*. Hoboken: John Wiley & Sons, Inc., 2012. Print.

Burton, Katherine. *Hedge Hunters: Hedge Fund Masters on the Rewards, the Risk, and the Reckoning*. New York: Bloomberg Press, 2007. Print.

Chung, Juliet. "Biggest Chapter Yet for a Poison Pen." *The Wall Street Journal*. Dow Jones & Company, Inc., 30 July 2012. Web. 6 September 2015.

Cohan, William D. "Little Big Man." *Vanity Fair*. Condé Nast, December 2013. Web. 6 September 2015.

"Daniel Loeb." *CNBC*. CNBC LLC, 6 October 2014. Web. 6 September 2015.

Demick, Barbara. "A Bankruptcy that Reached Beyond America's Borders: Wall Street's Most Famous Failure Hurt Banks that Trusted Drexel with Their Countries' Money." *The Philadelphia Inquirer*. Philadelphia Media Network, LLC, 19 January 1992. Web. 20 November 2015.

"Executive Team: Daniel S. Loeb." *Third Point*. Third Point LLC, n.d. Web. 6 September 2015.

Gandel, Stephen. "Dan Loeb Bashes Warren Buffett at Hedge Fund Conference." *Fortune*. Time Inc. Network, 6 May 2015. Web. 6 September 2015.

Gopinath, Deepak. "Hedge Fund Rabble Rouser." *Bloomberg Markets*. Bloomberg L.P., October 2005. Rpt. at ShookRun.com. ShookRun.com, n.d. Web. 6 September 2015.

Gross, Michael. *House of Outrageous Fortune: Fifteen Central Park West, the World's Most Powerful Address*. New York: Atria Paperback, a division of Simon & Schuster, Inc., 2014. Print.

Leibowitz, Ed. "Downtown 2.0: Cedd Moses." *Los Angeles Magazine*. Emmis Publishing, L.P., July 2008. Rpt. at *Seven Grand Bars*. 213 Spirited Ventures, LLC, n.d., Web. 20 November 2015.

"Malibu – Surfrider Beach." *Southern California Beaches*. Southern California Beaches, n.d. Web. 6 September 2015.

"Surfrider Foundation Announces Fifth Item in 'Treasures for the Coast Online Auction.'" *Surfrider Foundation*. Surfrider Foundation, n.d. Web. 6 September 2015.

"The World's Billionaires: #737 Daniel Loeb." *Forbes*. Forbes.com LLC, n.d. Web. 6 September 2015.

PETER LYNCH

Fisher, Anne. "From Golf Caddy to Big Shot: No Accidental Path." *Fortune*. Time Inc. Network, 17 July 2013. Web. 17 August 2015.

"How to Beat the Pros." *Changing Times*. The Kiplinger Washington Editors Inc., May 1989. Web. 17 August 2015.

"Lynch Dedication Is Nov. 2." *The Boston College Chronicle* Vol. 9, No. 4. The Boston College Chronicle, 19 October 2000. Web. 17 August 2015.

Lynch, Peter, and John Rothchild. *One Up On Wall Street: How to Use What You Already Know to Make Money in the Market*. New York: Simon & Schuster Paperbacks, 1989. Print.

"Peter S. Lynch, WG '68." *Wharton Alumni, University of Pennsylvania*. Wharton Club of New York, n.d. Web. 17 August 2015.

Reese, John P., and Jack M. Forehand. *The Guru Investor: How to Beat the Market Using History's Best Investment Strategies*. Hoboken: John Wiley & Sons, Inc., 2009. Print.

Schifrin, Matthew. "Peter Lynch: 10-Bagger Tales." *Forbes*. Forbes.com, LLC, 23 February 2009. Web. 17 August 2015.

"Stock Superstar Who Beat the Street: Peter S. Lynch, WG '68." *Wharton Alumni Magazine*. The Wharton School at the University of Pennsylvania, Spring 2007. Web. 17 August 2015.

Sullivan, Paul. "Peter Lynch Once Managed Money. Now He Gives It Away." *The New York Times*. The New York Times Company, 8 November 2013. Web. 17 August 2015.

Weiner, Eric J. *What Goes Up: The Uncensored History of Modern Wall Street as Told by the Bankers, Brokers, CEOs, and Scoundrels Who Made It Happen*. New York: Little, Brown and Company, 2005. Print.

HOWARD MARKS

"Howard Marks, Co-Chairman." *Oaktree*. Oaktree Capital Management, L.P., n.d. Web. 12 September 2015.

Kermond, Justin. "Howard Marks on Luck and Skill in Investing." *Advisor Perspectives*. Advisor Perspectives, Inc., 3 March 2015. Web. 12 September 2015.

Laing, Jonathan R. "Guru to the Stars." *Barron's*. Dow Jones & Company, Inc., 11 March 2013. Web. 12 September 2015.

Lattman, Peter. "Howard Marks's Missives, Now for the Masses." *The New York Times*. The New York Times Company, 12 May 2011. Web. 12 September 2015.

"Marks Family Writing Center, About Howard Marks." *The Critical Writing Program, Center for Programs in Contemporary Writing*. Center for Programs in Contemporary Writing, University of Pennsylvania, n.d. Web. 12 September 2015.

Maxfield, John. "A Warren Buffett Favorite Goes Public." *The Motley Fool*. The Motley Fool, 13 April 2012. Web. 12 September 2015.

"Money, Nerve, and a Lucky Birthday." *The Pennsylvania Gazette*. The Pennsylvania Gazette, 25 June 2014. Web. 12 September 2015.

Petruno, Tom. "L.A. Money Manager Oaktree Capital May List Shares on NYSE." *Los Angeles Times*. Los Angeles Times Media Group, 18 May 2011. Web. 12 September 2015.

Porter, Kiel. "Oaktree's Marks Says Europe Better Bet Than 'Highly Priced' U.S." *Bloomberg*. Bloomberg L.P., 21 May 2015. Web. 12 September 2015.

Wee, Gillian. "Biggest Distressed Debt Investor Marks Europe With 19% Gains." *Bloomberg*. Bloomberg L.P., 17 June 2011. Web. 12 September 2015.

MARK MOBIUS

"About Mark Mobius." *Investment Adventures in Emerging Markets*. Franklin Templeton Investments, n.d. Web. 12 September 2015.

Baker, Martin. "Business Profile: Perpetual Motion Mobius." *The Telegraph*. Telegraph Media Group Limited, 27 June 2004. Web. 13 September 2015.

Chan, Ronald. *The Value Investors: Lessons From the World's Top Fund Managers*. Singapore: John Wiley & Sons Singapore Pte. Ltd., 2012. Print.

"Eight Famous Ex-Americans." *The Wall Street Journal*. Dow Jones & Company, Inc., 18 May 2012. Web. 12 September 2015.

Evans, Richard. "Mark Mobius Quits the Helm of Templeton Emerging Markets." *The Telegraph*. Telegraph Media Group Limited, 13 July 2015. Web. 12 September 2015.

Gould, Carole. "Manager's Profile; J. Mark Mobius." *The New York Times*. The New York Times Company, 9 May 1993. Web. 12 September 2015.

"Mark Mobius: Man on the Go." *Silverkris*. Singapore Airlines Ltd. and SPH Magazines Pte. Ltd., 24 August 2014. Web. 13 September 2015.

Mobius, Mark. *Foreign Exchange: An Introduction to the Core Concepts*. Singapore: John Wiley & Sons (Asia) Pte. Ltd., 2008. Print.

Mobius, Mark. *Passport to Profits: Why the Next Investment Windfalls Will Be Found Abroad and How to Grab Your Share*. Singapore: John Wiley & Sons (Asia) Pte. Ltd., 2012. Print.

"The Face of Mammon." *The Economist*. The Economist Newspaper Limited, 2 December 1999. Web. 13 September 2015.

Xie, Ye. "The End of Mark Mobius's Reign as King of Emerging-Market Stocks." *Bloomberg*. Bloomberg L.P., 6 May 2015. Web. 12 September 2015.

CHARLIE MUNGER

DeMuth, Phil. "Charlie Munger's 2015 Daily Journal Annual Meeting—Part 1." *Forbes*. Forbes.com, LLC, 7 April 2015. Web. 18 August 2015.

Griffin, Tren. *Charlie Munger: The Complete Investor*. New York: Columbia University Press, 2015. Print.

Jordon, Steve. "Warren Buffett and Charlie Munger: Billion-Dollar Partnership." *Omaha.com*. Omaha World-Herald, 2 May 2015. Web. 18 August 2015.

Lowe, Janet. *Damn Right!: Behind the Scenes with Berkshire Hathaway Billionaire Charlie Munger*. Hoboken: John Wiley & Sons, Inc., 2000. Print.

"The World's Billionaires: #1415 Charles Munger." *Forbes*. Forbes.com LLC, n.d. Web. 18 August 2015.

JOHN NEFF

"Awards: Distinguished Alumni Award." *Weatherhead School of Management*. Weatherhead School of Management, Case Western Reserve University, n.d. Web. 15 September 2015.

Ellis, Charles D., and James R. Vertin. *Wall Street People: True Stories of Today's Masters and Moguls, Volume 2*. New York: John Wiley & Sons, Inc., 2001. Print.

Fuhrmann, Ryan. "Foolish Book Review: 'John Neff on Investing.'" *The Motley Fool*. The Motley Fool, 28 December 2006. Web. 15 September 2015.

Fuhrmann, Ryan. "John Neff, Legendary Investor: Part 2." *The Motley Fool*. The Motley Fool, 21 July 2006. Web. 15 September 2015.

Neff, John, and Steven L. Mintz. *John Neff on Investing*. New York: John Wiley & Sons, Inc., 1999. Print.

Reese, John P. "John Neff's Total Return P/E Approach." *Forbes*. Forbes.com, LLC, 1 June 2010. Web. 16 September 2015.

Reese, John P. "Six Stocks Famed Vanguard Windsor Manager John Neff Would Like." *Forbes*. Forbes.com, LLC, 12 April 2011. Web. 15 September 2015.

Rublin, Lauren R. "John Neff's History Class." *Barron's*. Dow Jones & Company, Inc., 23 September 2002. Web. 15 September 2015.

Strunk, Jon. "Wall Street Legend Invests $4 Million in UT College of Business Administration." *UToday*. The University of Toledo, 15 June 2007. Web. 15 September 2015.

BILL NYGREN

"Bill Nygren." *Stocks 500*. Morningstar, Inc., n.d. Web. 16 September 2015.

Kays, Scott. *Five Key Lessons from Top Money Managers*. Hoboken: John Wiley & Sons, Inc., 2005. Print.

Marte, Jonnelle. "Are Stock Markets Near 'Dangerous Territory?'" *The Washington Post*. The Washington Post, 31 July 2015. Web. 8 August 2015.

"Morningstar Hall of Fame: Fund Manager of the Year Winners." *Morningstar*. Morningstar, Inc., n.d. Web. 16 September 2015.

"Portfolio Managers." *Harris Associates*. Harris Associates, n.d. Web. 16 September 2015.

Sahadi, Jeanne. "Vexed By Varsity, Not Value: Baseball, Buffett and His Folks Help Make Oakmark's Bill Nygren a Success." *CNN Money*. Cable News Network, A Time Warner Company, 30 May 2000. Web. 16 September 2015.

"Statement of Additional Information." *Oakmark Funds*. Harris Associates Securities L.P., 28 January 2015. Web. 16 September 2015.

Strauss, Lawrence. "Paying a Bit More For a Lot More Value." *Barron's*. Dow Jones & Company, Inc., 31 July 2001. Web. 16 September 2015.

MOHNISH PABRAI

"Bio: Mohnish Pabrai." *South Asian Business Association*. UCLA Anderson School of Management, n.d. Web. 18 August 2015.

"Events: April 2, 2013, Hedge Fund Manager Mohnish Pabrai." *Graduate Finance Association*. Boston College, n.d. Web. 18 August 2015.

Kimelman, John. "Buffett Disciple Mohnish Pabrai on Bank of America, Citi, Google, and Hyundai." *Barron's*. Dow Jones & Company, Inc., 9 December 2014. Web. 18 August 2015.

Levinson, Meridith. "The Rise & Fall of Digital Disrupters or the Entrepreneur's Dilemma." *CIO*. CXO Media Inc., 15 January 2001. Web. 18 August 2015.

Murcko, Tom. "Interview With Value Investor Mohnish Pabrai." *InvestorGuide.com*. WebFinance, Inc., n.d. Web. 18 August 2015.

Pabrai, Mohnish. *The Dhandho Investor: The Low-Risk Value Method to High Returns*. Hoboken: John Wiley & Sons, Inc., 2007. Print.

Proctor, William, and Scott Phillips. *The Templeton Touch*. West Conshohocken: Templeton Press, 2012. Print.

Spier, Guy. *The Education of a Value Investor: My Transformative Quest for Wealth, Wisdom, and Enlightenment*. New York: Palgrave Macmillan Trade, 2014. Print.

Touryalai, Halah. "Turning Slumdogs Into Millionaires: One Hedge Fund Manager's Quest." *Forbes*. Forbes.com, LLC, 25 June 2012. Web. 18 August 2015.

Zendrian, Alexandra. "Get Briefed: Mohnish Pabrai." *Forbes*. Forbes.com, LLC, 12 April 2010. Web. 18 August 2015.

JOHN PAULSON

"John Paulson Fast Facts." *CNN*. Cable News Network, Turner Broadcasting System, Inc., 11 March 2015. Web. 19 August 2015.

"John Paulson." *Paulson & Co. Inc*. Paulson & Co. Inc., n.d. Web. 19 August 2015.

Zuckerman, Gregory. *The Greatest Trade Ever: The Behind-the-Scenes Story of How John Paulson Defied Wall Street and Made Financial History*. New York: Crown Business, 2010, 2009. Print.

Zuckerman, Gregory. "Trader Made Billions on Subprime." *The Wall Street Journal*. Dow Jones & Company, Inc., 15 January 2008. Web. 19 August 2015.

NELSON PELTZ

"About Us: Trian Overview and History." *Trian Partners*. Trian Fund Management, L.P., n.d. Web. 16 September 2015.

Bhaktavatsalam, Sree Vidya. "Legg Mason Rises on Report Peltz May Push for Sale (Update 2)." *Bloomberg*. Bloomberg L.P., 24 June 2009. Web. 16 September 2015.

Burton, Katherine, and Sree Vidya Bhaktavatsalam. "Nelson Peltz Is Still Scaring Companies." *Bloomberg*. Bloomberg L.P., 27 September 2012. Web. 16 September 2015.

Burton, Katherine, and Sree Vidya Bhaktavatsalam. "Peltz Gets $1 Billion as Activist Strategy Impresses." *Bloomberg*. Bloomberg L.P., 20 September 2012. Web. 16 September 2015.

"Business People; Sale Won't End Career of Peltz Food's Owner." *The New York Times*. The New York Times Company, 26 August 1988. Web. 16 September 2015.

Jargon, Julie. "A Bite at a Time, Peltz Reshapes Food Industry." *The Wall Street Journal*. Dow Jones & Company, Inc., 7 November 2007. Web. 16 September 2015.

McCracken, Jeffrey, and Laura Marcinek. "Peltz Said to Have Pressed Lazard on Cutting Banker Compensation." *Bloomberg*. Bloomberg L.P., 21 June 2012. Web. 16 September 2015.

Mulligan, Thomas S., and Martin Zimmerman. "Peltz Is Cagey on Tribune Investment." *Los Angeles Times*. Los Angeles Times, 21 August 2006. Web. 16 September 2016.

Sellers, Patricia. "Corporate Raider Nelson Peltz Simply Can't Resist Women." *Fortune*. Time Inc. Network, 12 January 2015. Web. 16 September 2015.

Thomas, Rob, and Patrick McSharry. *Big Data Revolution: What Farmers, Doctors and Insurance Agents Teach Us About Discovering Big Data Patterns*. Chichester: John Wiley & Sons Ltd., 2015. Print.

RICHARD RAINWATER

Bancroft, Bill. "A Texas Power Play." *The New York Times*. The New York Times Company, 11 June 1989. Web. 26 September 2015.

Burke, Doris. "Sittin' Pretty Texas Investor Richard Rainwater Believed in Oil When Everyone Else Was Infatuated With Technology. He Made a Ton of Money—And Says You Can Too." *Fortune*. Time Inc. Network, 11 June 2011. Web. 27 September 2015.

Burrough, Bryan. *The Big Rich: The Rise and Fall of the Greatest Texas Oil Fortunes*. New York: Penguin Group (USA) Inc., 2009. Print.

"Classmates Heap Praise on Rainwater." *Stanford Graduate School of Business*. Stanford Graduate School of Business, n.d. Web. 17 September 2015.

Elkind, Peter, and Patricia Sellers. "Richard Rainwater: Remembering a Billionaire Dealmaker." *Fortune*. Time Inc. Network, 28 September 2015. Web. 9 November 2015.

Elkind, Peter, et al. "The Fight of Richard Rainwater's Life." *Fortune*. Time Inc. Network, 7 November 2011. Web. 27 September 2015.

Forest, Stephanie Anderson, et al. "Rainwater, Can He Recoup?" *Business Week*. Bloomberg L.P., 30 November 1998. Web. 17 September 2015.

Hollandsworth, Skip. "Richard Rainwater, The Invisible Man Behind One of the Year's Biggest Deals." *Texas Monthly*. Texas Monthly, September 1996. Web. 17 September 2015.

Maggard, Margaret. *Guide to Private Fortunes, 1993*. Rockville: The Taft Group, 1993. Print.

"Profile: Richard Rainwater." *Bloomberg*. Bloomberg L.P., n.d. Web. 17 September 2015.

Train, John. *Money Masters of Our Time*. New York: HarperCollins Publishers Inc., 2000. Print.

RENE RIVKIN

Ansley, Greg. "Fall of Australia's Guru of Greed." *The New Zealand Herald*. NZME Publishing Limited, 17 January 2004. Web. 10 October 2015.

Askew, Kate. "Trade Winds Blow Cold." *The Age*. The Age Company Ltd, 3 May 2003. Web. 9 October 2015.

Chenoweth, Neil. *Packer's Lunch*. Crows Nest: Allen & Unwin, 2007. Print.

Cox, Kate. "Rene's Free and Easy." *The Sydney Morning Herald*. The Sydney Morning Herald, 1 June 2003. Web. 9 October 2015.

Day, Selina. "Stock Tips, Cigars and Worry Beads." *The Age*. The Age Company Ltd, 2 May 2005. Web. 9 October 2015.

Main, Andrew. *Rivkin Unauthorised: The Meteoric Rise and Tragic Fall of an Unorthodox Money Man*. Sydney: HarperCollinsPublishers Pty Limited, 2005. Print.

McClymont, Kate, and Jordan Baker. "Sad End for Rene Rivkin." *The Sydney Morning Herald*. The Sydney Morning Herald, 2 May 2005. Web. 28 September 2015.

McClymont, Kate. "'Do You Think I Did It?' The $20,000 Question the Jury Never Heard." *The Sydney Morning Herald*. The Sydney Morning Herald, 22 November 2008. Web. 9 October 2015.

McClymont, Kate. "Eddie Obeid's 'Likely' $1M Share of Offset Alpine Payout." *The Sydney Morning Herald*. The Sydney Morning Herald, 30 July 2014. Web. 9 October 2015.

McClymont, Kate. "For Some, a Tidy Payout Hot Off the Presses." *The Age*. The Age Company Ltd, 31 October 2003. Web. 9 October 2015.

McIntyre, Paul. "The Rise and Fall of Rene Rivkin." *The New Zealand Herald*. NZME Publishing Limited, 6 May 2005. Web. 1 October 2015.

Moran, Susannah. "Rene Rivkin Fortunes are Lost Forever." *The Australian*. Nationwide News Pty Limited, 16 April 2013. Web. 28 September 2015.

Mychasuk, Emiliya. "Making a Buck in Alpine Country." *The Age*. The Age Company Ltd, 12 June 2004. Web. 9 October 2015.

"Rene Rivkin Dead." *ABC News*. The Australian Broadcasting Corporation, 1 May 2005. Web. 28 September 2015.

Smith, Matthew. "Rivkin 2.0: Sons Dial Down the Bravado." *BRW*. Fairfax Media Publications Pty Ltd, 01 February 2013. Web. 9 October 2015.

Verrender, Ian. "Pity the Poor Man." *The Sydney Morning Herald*. The Sydney Morning Herald, 3 May 2005. Web. 9 October 2015.

LARRY ROBBINS

Arvedlund, Erin E. "Bullish on Obamacare." *Barron's*. Dow Jones & Company, Inc., 27 July 2013. Web. 12 October 2015.

"Larry Robbins." *The Wharton Club of New York*. Wharton Club of New York, n.d. Web. 12 October 2015.

"The Forbes 400 List of the Richest Americans: #182 Leon G. Cooperman." *Forbes*. Forbes.com LLC, 29 September 2015. Web. 12 October 2015.

"The Forbes 400 List of the Richest Americans: #293 Larry Robbins." *Forbes*. Forbes.com LLC, 29 September 2015. Web. 12 October 2015.

"The Next List: Larry Robbins." *CNBC*. CNBC LLC, 6 October 2014. Web. 12 October 2015.

Toscano. Paul. "Stocks Still Great for Long-Term Investors: Larry Robbins." *CNBC*. CNBC LLC, 25 June 2013. Web. 12 October 2015.

Whitehouse, Kaja. "A Rebound for Hedgie Robbins." *New York Post*. NYP Holdings, Inc. 2 January 2013. Web. 12 October 2015.

CHARLES M. ROYCE

"About: A Style Cultivated Over Four Decades." *Royce Funds*. Royce & Associates, LLC, n.d. Web. 17 October 2015.

"About: Investment Approach." *Royce Funds*. Royce & Associates, LLC, n.d. Web. 17 October 2015.

Brill, Marla. "Royce's Goal: Safety First." *Financial Advisor Magazine*. Charter Financial Publishing Network Inc., 1 October 2001. Web. 18 October 2015.

"Chuck Royce Featured in WSJ's Article 'Funds Prepare for Eventual Succession.'" *Royce Funds*. Royce & Associates, LLC, n.d. Web. 18 October 2015.

Goodman, Beverly. "Can Legg Mason Bounce Back?" *Barron's*. Dow Jones & Company, Inc., 9 April 2012. Web. 13 October 2015.

Kidwell, Sarah. "Brown Corporation Elects Three New Fellows and Six New Trustees." *News from Brown*. Brown University, 28 May 2010. Web. 17 October 2015.

"People: Chuck Royce." *Royce Funds*. Royce & Associates, LLC, n.d. Web. 17 October 2015.

Rosenberg, Yuval. "Ultimate Fund Portfolio." *Fortune*. Time Inc. Network, 14 June 2007. Web. 18 October 2015.

Weiss, Stephen L. *The Big Win: Learning from the Legends to Become a More Successful Investor*. Hoboken: John Wiley & Sons, Inc., 2012. Print.

WALTER SCHLOSS

Arnold, Laurence. "Walter Schloss, 'Superinvestor' Praised by Buffett, Dies at 95." *Bloomberg*. Bloomberg L.P., 20 February 2012. Web. 17 September 2015.

Condon, Bernard. "Experience." *Forbes*. Forbes.com, LLC, 11 February 2008. Web. 17 October 2015.

Rabinowich, Eli. "Going Out on Top: Walter & Edwin Schloss." *Bottom Line*. Columbia University, 17 April 2003. Rpt. at Graham and Doddsville, SuperInvestor Resources. *Graham and Doddsville*, n.d. Web. 17 October 2015.

Schloss, Walter. "Why We Invest the Way We Do." Behavioral Economics Forum. Harvard Faculty Club, Cambridge, MA. 16 May 1996. Lecture. Rpt. at Elevation Capital, Walter Schloss Archives. *Elevation Capital Management Limited*, n.d. Web. 17 October 2015.

Welling, Kathryn M. "The Right Stuff: Why Walter Schloss is Such a Great Investor." *Barron's*. Dow Jones & Company, Inc., 25 February 1985. Rpt. at Graham and Doddsville, SuperInvestor Resources. *Graham and Doddsville*, n.d. Web. 15 October 2015.

LOU SIMPSON

Barboza, David. "GEICO Chief May Be Heir to a Legend." *The New York Times*. The New York Times Company, 29 April 1997. Web. 17 September 2015.

"Executive Profile: Louis A. Simpson." *Bloomberg*. Bloomberg L.P., n.d. Web. 17 September 2015.

Harris, Melissa. "Lou Simpson Retiring from GEICO." *Chicago Tribune*. Tribune Publishing Company, 22 August 2010. Web. 17 September 2015.

Miles, Robert P. *The Warren Buffett CEO: Secrets from the Berkshire Hathaway Managers*. New York: John Wiley & Sons, Inc., 2002. Print.

Vise, David A. "GEICO'S Top Market Strategist Churning Out Profits." *The Washington Post*. The Washington Post, 11 May 1987. Web. 21 October 2015.

Weiss, Miles. "Buffett Stock Picker Simpson Opens Own Firm After Leaving GEICO." *Bloomberg*. Bloomberg L.P., 21 January 2011. Web. 17 September 2015.

GEORGE SOROS

"About George Soros." *Open Society Georgia Foundation*. Open Society—Georgia Foundation, n.d. Web. 19 August 2015.

Clark, Nicola. "Soros Loses Challenge to Insider Trading Conviction." *The New York Times*. The New York Times Company, 6 October 2011. Web. 27 November 2015.

"Company Overview of Soros Fund Management LLC." *Bloomberg*. Bloomberg L.P., n.d. Web. 27 November 2015.

"George Soros: Books." *George Soros*. GeorgeSoros.com, n.d. Web. 21 August 2015.

"Insider Trading Conviction of Soros is Upheld." *International Herald Tribune*. The New York Times Company, 14 June 2006. Web. 22 November 2015.

Kaufman, Michael T. *Soros: The Life and Times of a Messianic Billionaire*. New York: Alfred A. Knopf, a division of Random House Inc., 2002. Print.

Litterick, David. "Billionaire Who Broke the Bank of England." *The Telegraph*. Telegraph Media Group Limited, 13 September 2002. Web. 19 August 2015.

Lynch, David J. "Soros Sees 'Reflexivity' Theory of Economics as Life's Work." *USA Today*. USA TODAY, a division of Gannett Co. Inc., 13 May 2008. Web. 21 August 2015.

Soros, George. "Soros: General Theory of Reflexivity." *Financial Times*. The Financial Times Limited, 26 October 2009. Web. 21 August 2015.

Soros, George. *Soros on Soros: Staying Ahead of the Curve*. New York: John Wiley & Sons, Inc., 1995. Print.

"The Man Who Moves Markets." *Bloomberg*. Bloomberg L.P., 22 August 1993. Web. 19 August 2015.

JOHN TEMPLETON

Friedman, Josh. "Investment Pioneer Funded Spiritual Efforts." *Los Angeles Times*. Los Angeles Times, 9 July 2008. Web. 24 August 2015.

Herrmann, Robert L. *Sir John Templeton: From Wall Street to Humility Theology*. Radnor: Templeton Foundation Press, 2004, 1998. Rpt. at *Sir John Templeton*. Sir John Templeton, n.d. Web. 24 August 2015.

Laise, Eleanor. "Interview With Sir John Templeton." *SmartMoney*. SmartMoney, 1 April 2004. Rpt. at *Sir John Templeton*. Sir John Templeton, n.d. Web. 24 August 2015.

"Life Story." *John Templeton Foundation*. John Templeton Foundation, n.d. Web. 23 August 2015.

"Milestones in the Life of Sir John Templeton." *Sir John Templeton*. Sir John Templeton, n.d. Web. 24 August 2015.

"Photographs." *Sir John Templeton*. Sir John Templeton, n.d. Web. 24 August 2015.

Proctor, William, and Scott Phillips. *The Templeton Touch*. West Conshohocken: Templeton Press, 2012. Print.

Scott, George Cole. "Sir John Templeton and Dr. Mark Mobius on Emerging Markets." *The Scott Letter: Closed-End Fund Report*. Closed-End Fund Advisors, Inc., January 2002. Web. 24 August 2015.

"The Joy of Giving: Sir John's Vision for a Better World." *John Templeton Foundation*. John Templeton Foundation, n.d. Web. 30 August 2015.

DAVID TEPPER

Ahuja, Maneet. *The Alpha Masters: Unlocking the Genius of the World's Top Hedge Funds*. Hoboken: John Wiley & Sons, Inc., 2012. Print.

Caplinger, Dan. "Should You Own David Tepper's 3 Favorite Stocks?" *The Motley Fool*. The Motley Fool, 22 November 2015. Web. 27 November 2015.

Chute, Eleanor. "CMU Graduate David A. Tepper Gives His School $67 Million." *Pittsburgh Post-Gazette*. PG Publishing Co., Inc., 15 November 2013. Web. 30 August 2015.

Lane, Jackson. "David Tepper Earns $7 Billion." *The Tartan: Carnegie Mellon's Student Newspaper Since 1906*. The Tartan, 18 January 2010. Web. 23 August 2015.

Pressler, Jessica. "Ready to Be Rich." *New York Magazine*. New York Media LLC, 26 September 2010. Web. 30 August 2015.

"The Richest Person in Every State: David Tepper." *Forbes*. Forbes.com LLC, n.d. Web. 30 August 2015.

"Topics: David Tepper." *The Wall Street Journal*. Dow Jones & Company, Inc., n.d. Web. 1 September 2015.

PREM WATSA

Castaldo, Joe. "The Man With Nothing to Lose." *Canadian Business*. Rogers Media, 10 October 2013. Web. 2 September 2015.

"Company Profile." *Fairfax Financial Holdings Limited*. Fairfax Financial Holdings Limited, n.d. Web. 1 September 2015.

"Discover Ivey: History." *Ivey Business School*. Ivey Business School, Western University, n.d. Web. 2 September 2015.

"Executive Profile: V. Prem Watsa." *Bloomberg*. Bloomberg L.P., n.d. Web. 2 September 2015.

Hopkins, Andrea, and Cameron French. "BlackBerry Savior Watsa, an Investor With a Long View." *Reuters*. Thomson Reuters, 23 September 2013. Web. 2 September 2015.

Kuitenbrouwer, Peter. "Fairfax Financial Ltd Chief Prem Watsa Tells His 'Horatio Alger' Story." *Financial Post*. National Post, a divison of Postmedia Network Inc., 22 May 2015. Web. 2 September 2015.

Ligaya, Armina. "BlackBerry Ltd Backer Prem Watsa Bets Big on Bailed-Out Greek Bank, Europe Turnaround." *Financial Post*. National Post, a divison of Postmedia Network Inc., 15 April 2014. Web. 2 September 2015.

Pasternak, Sean B., and Hugo Miller. "Watsa, Who Models Buffett, Sees Housing Bubble: Corporate Canada." *Bloomberg*. Bloomberg L.P., 27 April 2012. Web. 2 September 2015.

Peterson-Withorn, Chase. "Rising Fairfax Financial Stocks Make 'Canada's Warren Buffett' a Billionaire." *Forbes*. Forbes.com, LLC, 3 December 2014. Web. 1 September 2015.

MARTIN J. WHITMAN

"About Whitman." *Forbes*. Forbes.com LLC, 11 April 2009. Web. 6 September 2015.

Brown, Abram. "Stock Picks And Investing Wisdom From Value Guru Marty Whitman." *Forbes*. Forbes.com, LLC, 5 June 2013. Web. 30 November 2015.

Buzzell, Dave. "Whitman to Receive Miller Award." *Turnarounds & Workouts* 27. 11 (November 2013): 1, 2, 4, 6. Rpt. at *Mesirow Financial*. Mesirow Financial Holdings, Inc., n.d., Web. 6 September 2015.

"History." *Third Avenue Management*. Third Avenue Management, LLC, n.d. Web. 4 September 2015.

"Martin J. Whitman, CFA." *Third Avenue Management*. Third Avenue Management, LLC, n.d. Web. 4 September 2015.

"Martin J. Whitman—Veteran and Syracuse University Faculty Alumnus." *Syracuse University Institute for Veterans and Military Families*. Syracuse University IVMF at Barclay, n.d. Web. 4 September 2015.

Rabinowich, Eli. "Martin J. Whitman: Economic vs. Academic Reality." *Bottom Line*. Columbia University, 22 April 2004. Rpt. at Graham and Doddsville, SuperInvestor Resources. *Graham and Doddsville*, n.d. Web. 5 September 2015.

Rosenberg, Hilary. *The Vulture Investors*. New York: John Wiley & Sons, Inc., 1992, 2000. Print.

Weiss, Stephen L. *The Big Win: Learning from the Legends to Become a More Successful Investor*. Hoboken: John Wiley & Sons, Inc., 2012. Print.

"Whitman History: Martin J. Whitman." *Whitman School of Management, Syracuse University*. Whitman School of Management, n.d. Web. 4 September 2015.

DONALD YACKTMAN

Cendrowski, Scott. "Don Yacktman: A Fund Manager's Faith Produces Results." *Fortune*. Time Inc. Network, 13 December 2012. Web. 7 September 2015.

"Investment Team: Donald Yacktman." *Yacktman Asset Management*. Yacktman Asset Management LP, n.d. Web. 7 September 2015.

Kazanjian, Kirk. *Growing Rich with Growth Stocks: Wall Street's Top Money Managers Reveal the 12 Rules for Investment Success*. New York: New York Institute of Finance, a Simon & Schuster Company, 1999. Print.

"Part 2A of Form ADV: Yacktman Asset Management Co." *Lexis Securities Mosaic*. LexisNexis., 31 March 2011. Web. 8 September 2015

"Profiles: Donald 'Don' Yacktman." *Bloomberg*. Bloomberg L.P., n.d. Web. 7 September 2015.

Shari, Michael. "Keeping His Distance." *Barron's*. Dow Jones & Company, Inc., 22 May 2010. Web. 11 September 2015.

Strauss, Lawrence C. "Redemption." *Barron's*. Dow Jones & Company, Inc., 26 January 2004. Web. 7 September 2015.

CPSIA information can be obtained
at www.ICGtesting.com
Printed in the USA
BVHW040001280820
587520BV00012B/323